William Makepeace Thackeray

The four Georges

Sketches of Manners, Morals, Court and Town Life

William Makepeace Thackeray

The four Georges
Sketches of Manners, Morals, Court and Town Life

ISBN/EAN: 9783743310728

Manufactured in Europe, USA, Canada, Australia, Japa

Cover: Foto ©Thomas Meinert / pixelio.de

Manufactured and distributed by brebook publishing software
(www.brebook.com)

William Makepeace Thackeray

The four Georges

A little Rebel.

THE FOUR GEORGES:

BY

W. M. THACKERAY,

AUTHOR OF "LECTURES ON THE ENGLISH HUMOURISTS,"
ETC. ETC.

WITH ILLUSTRATIONS

LONDON:

SMITH, ELDER AND CO., 65, CORNHILL.

M.DCCC.LXI.

I.—GEORGE THE FIRST.

GEORGE THE FIRST.

VERY few years since, I knew familiarly a lady, who had been asked in marriage by Horace Walpole, who had been patted on the head by George I. This lady had knocked at Dr. Johnson's door; had been intimate with Fox, the beautiful Georgina

Note.—The initial letter is from an old Dutch print of Herrenhausen.

of Devonshire, and that brilliant Whig society
of the reign of George III.; had known the
Duchess of Queensberry, the patroness of Gay
and Prior, the admired young beauty of the court
of Queen Anne. I often thought as I took my
kind old friend's hand, how with it I held on to
the old society of wits and men of the world. I
could travel back for seven score years of time
—have glimpses of Brummell, Selwyn, Chesterfield and the men of pleasure; of Walpole
and Conway; of Johnson, Reynolds, Goldsmith; of North, Chatham, Newcastle; of the
fair maids of honour of George II.'s court; of
the German retainers of George I.'s; where
Addison was secretary of state; where Dick
Steele held a place; whither the great Marlborough came with his fiery spouse; when Pope,
and Swift, and Bolingbroke yet lived and wrote.
Of a society so vast, busy, brilliant, it is impossible in four brief chapters to give a complete
notion; but we may peep here and there into
that bygone world of the Georges, see what they
and their courts were like; glance at the people
round about them; look at past manners, fashions,
pleasures, and contrast them with our own. I have

to say thus much by way of preface, because the subject of these lectures has been misunderstood, and I have been taken to task for not having given grave historical treatises, which it never was my intention to attempt. Not about battles, about politics, about statesmen and measures of state, did I ever think to lecture you : but to sketch the manners and life of the old world ; to amuse for a few hours with talk about the old society ; and, with the result of many a day's and night's pleasant reading, to try and wile away a few winter evenings for my hearers.

Among the German princes who sate under Luther at Wittenberg, was Duke Ernest of Celle, whose younger son, William of Lüneburg, was the progenitor of the illustrious Hanoverian house at present reigning in Great Britain. Duke William held his court at Celle, a little town of ten thousand people that lies on the railway line between Hamburg and Hanover, in the midst of great plains of sand, upon the river Aller. When Duke William had it, it was a very humble wood-built place, with a great brick church, which he sedulously frequented, and in which he and others

of his house lie buried. He was a very religious
lord, and called William the Pious by his small
circle of subjects, over whom he ruled till fate
deprived him both of sight and reason. Sometimes, in his latter days, the good duke had
glimpses of mental light, when he would bid his
musicians play the psalm-tunes which he loved.
One thinks of a descendant of his, two hundred
years afterwards, blind, old, and lost of wits,
singing Handel in Windsor Tower.

William the Pious had fifteen children, eight
daughters and seven sons, who, as the property
left among them was small, drew lots to deter-
mine which one of them should marry, and con-
tinue the stout race of the Guelphs. The lot
fell on Duke George, the sixth brother. The
others remained single, or contracted left-handed
marriages after the princely fashion of those days.
It is a queer picture—that of the old prince dying
in his little wood-built capital, and his seven sons
tossing up which should inherit and transmit the
crown of Brentford. Duke George, the lucky prize-
man, made the tour of Europe, during which he
visited the court of Queen Elizabeth; and in the
year 1617, came back and settled at Zell, with a

wife out of Darmstadt. His remaining brothers
all kept their house at Zell, for economy's sake.
And presently, in due course, they all died—all
the honest dukes; Ernest, and Christian, and
Augustus, and Magnus, and George, and John—
and they are buried in the brick church of Brentford yonder, by the sandy banks of the Aller.

Dr. Vehse gives a pleasant glimpse of the way
of life of our dukes in Zell. "When the trumpeter
on the tower has blown," Duke Christian orders
—viz. at nine o'clock in the morning, and four
in the evening, every one must be present at
meals, and those who are not must go without.
None of the servants, unless it be a knave who
has been ordered to ride out, shall eat or drink
in the kitchen or cellar; or, without special leave,
fodder his horses at the prince's cost. When
the meal is served in the court-room, a page
shall go round and bid every one be quiet and
orderly, forbidding all cursing, swearing, and
rudeness; all throwing about of bread, bones,
or roast, or pocketing of the same. Every morning, at seven, the squires shall have their morning
soup, along with which, and dinner, they shall be
served with their under-drink—every morning,

except Friday morning, when there was sermon, and no drink. Every evening they shall have their beer, and at night their sleep-drink. The butler is especially warned not to allow noble or simple to go into the cellar: wine shall only be served at the prince's or councillor's table; and every Monday, the honest old Duke Christian ordains the accounts shall be ready, and the expenses in the kitchen, the wine and beer cellar, the bakehouse and stable, made out.

Duke George, the marrying duke, did not stop at home to partake of the beer and wine, and the sermons. He went about fighting wherever there was profit to be had. He served as general in the army of the circle of Lower Saxony, the Protestant army; then he went over to the emperor, and fought in his armies in Germany and Italy; and when Gustavus Adolphus appeared in Germany, George took service as a Swedish general, and seized the Abbey of Hildesheim, as his share of the plunder. Here, in the year 1641, Duke George died, leaving four sons behind him, from the youngest of whom descend our royal Georges.

Under these children of Duke George, the old

God-fearing, simple ways of Zell appear to have gone out of mode. The second brother was constantly visiting Venice, and leading a jolly, wicked life there. It was the most jovial of all places at the end of the seventeenth century; and military men, after a campaign, rushed thither, as the warriors of the Allies rushed to Paris in 1814, to gamble, and rejoice, and partake of all sorts of godless delights. This prince, then, loving Venice and its pleasures, brought Italian singers and dancers back with him to quiet old Zell; and, worse still, demeaned himself by marrying a French lady of birth quite inferior to his own— Eleanor D'Olbreuse, from whom our queen is descended. Eleanor had a pretty daughter, who inherited a great fortune, which inflamed her cousin, George Louis of Hanover, with a desire to marry her; and so, with her beauty and her riches, she came to a sad end.

It is too long to tell how the four sons of Duke George divided his territories amongst them, and how, finally, they came into possession of the son of the youngest of the four. In this generation the Protestant faith was very nearly extinguished in the family: and then where should we in

England have gone for a king? The third brother
also took delight in Italy, where the priests con-
verted him and his Protestant chaplain too.
Mass was said in Hanover once more; and Italian
soprani piped their Latin rhymes in place of the
hymns which William the Pious and Dr. Luther
sang. Louis XIV. gave this and other converts
a splendid pension. Crowds of Frenchmen and
brilliant French fashions came into his court. It
is incalculable how much that royal bigwig cost
Germany. Every prince imitated the French
king, and had his Versailles, his Wilhelmshöhe
or Ludwigslust; his court and its splendours;
his gardens laid out with statues; his fountains,
and water-works, and Tritons; his actors, and
dancers, and singers, and fiddlers; his harem, with
its inhabitants; his diamonds and duchies for
these latter; his enormous festivities, his gaming-
tables, tournaments, masquerades, and banquets
lasting a week long, for which the people paid
with their money, when the poor wretches had it;
with their bodies and very blood when they had
none; being sold in thousands by their lords and
masters, who gaily dealt in soldiers, staked a regiment upon the red at the gambling-table; swapped

a battalion against a dancing-girl's diamond neck-
lace; and, as it were, pocketed their people.

As one views Europe, through contemporary
books of travel in the early part of the last century,
the landscape is awful—wretched wastes, beggarly
and plundered; half-burned cottages and trembling peasants gathering piteous harvests; gangs
of such tramping along with bayonets behind
them, and corporals with canes and cats-of-nine-
tails to flog them to barracks. By these passes
my lord's gilt carriage floundering through the
ruts, as he swears at the postilions, and toils on
to the Residenz. Hard by, but away from the
noise and brawling of the citizens and buyers, is
Wilhelmslust or Ludwigsruhe, or Monbijou, or
Versailles—it scarcely matters which,—near to
the city, shut out by woods from the beggared
country, the enormous, hideous, gilded, monstrous marble palace, where the prince is, and the
Court, and the trim gardens, and huge fountains,
and the forest where the ragged peasants are
beating the game in (it is death to them to touch
a feather); and the jolly hunt sweeps by with its
uniform of crimson and gold; and the prince
gallops ahead puffing his royal horn; and his

lords and mistresses ride after him; and the stag
is pulled down; and the grand huntsman gives
the knife in the midst of a chorus of bugles; and
'tis time the Court go home to dinner; and our
noble traveller, it may be the Baron of Pöllnitz,
or the Count de Königsmarck, or the excellent
Chevalier de Seingalt, sees the procession gleam-
ing through the trim avenues of the wood, and
hastens to the inn, and sends his noble name to
the marshal of the Court. Then our nobleman
arrays himself in green and gold, or pink and
silver, in the richest Paris mode, and is introduced by the chamberlain, and makes his bow to
the jolly prince, and the gracious princess; and
is presented to the chief lords and ladies, and
then comes supper and a bank at Faro, where he
loses or wins a thousand pieces by daylight. If it
is a German court, you may add not a little
drunkenness to this picture of high life; but
German, or French, or Spanish, if you can see
out of your palace-windows beyond the trim-cut
forest vistas, misery is lying outside; hunger is
stalking about the bare villages, listlessly following precarious husbandry; ploughing stony fields
with starved cattle; or fearfully taking in scanty

harvests. Augustus is fat and jolly on his throne;
he can knock down an ox, and eat one almost;
his mistress Aurora von Königsmarck is the love-
liest, the wittiest creature; his diamonds are the
biggest and most brilliant in the world, and his
feasts as splendid as those of Versailles. As for
Louis the Great, he is more than mortal. Lift
up your glances respectfully, and mark him eyeing
Madame de Fontanges or Madame de Montespan
from under his **sublime** periwig, **as** he passes
through the great gallery where Villars and Ven-
dome, and Berwick, and Bossuet, and Massillon
are waiting. Can Court be more splendid; nobles
and knights more gallant and superb; ladies
more lovely? A grander monarch, or a more
miserable starved wretch than the peasant his
subject, you cannot look on. Let us bear both
these types in mind, if we wish to estimate the
old society properly. Remember the glory and
the chivalry? Yes! Remember the grace and
beauty, the splendour and lofty politeness; the
gallant courtesy of Fontenoy, where the French
line bids the gentlemen of the English guard to
fire first; the noble constancy of the old king
and Villars his general, who fits out the last army

with the last crown-piece from the treasury, and
goes to meet the enemy and die or conquer for
France at Denain. But round all that royal
splendour lies a nation enslaved and ruined:
there are people robbed of their rights—communi-
ties laid waste—faith, justice, commerce trampled
upon, and well-nigh destroyed—nay, in the very
centre of royalty itself, what horrible stains and
meanness, crime and shame! It is but to a silly
harlot that some of the noblest gentlemen, and
some of the proudest women in the world, are
bowing down; it is the price of a miserable province that the king ties in diamonds round his
mistress's white neck. In the first half of the
last century, I say, this is going on all Europe
over. Saxony is a waste as well as Picardy or
Artois; and Versailles is only larger and not
worse than Herrenhausen.

It was the first Elector of Hanover who made
the fortunate match which bestowed the race of
Hanoverian Sovereigns upon us Britons. Nine
years after Charles Stuart lost his head, his niece
Sophia, one of many children of another luckless
dethroned sovereign, the Elector Palatine, married
Ernest Augustus of Brunswick, and brought the

reversion to the crown of the three kingdoms in her scanty trousseau. One of the handsomest, the most cheerful, sensible, shrewd, accomplished of

women, was Sophia,* daughter of poor Frederick, the winter king of Bohemia. The other daughters

* The above portraits are from contemporary prints of this princess, before her marriage, and in her old age.

of lovely, unhappy Elizabeth Stuart went off into
the Catholic Church ; this one, luckily for her
family, remained, I cannot say faithful to the
Reformed Religion, but at least she adopted no
other. An agent of the French king's, Gourville,
a convert himself, strove to bring her and her
husband to a sense of the truth ; and tells us that
he one day asked Madame the Duchess of Hanover, of what religion her daughter was, then a
pretty girl of thirteen years old. The duchess
replied that the princess *was of no religion as yet.*
They were waiting to know of what religion her
husband would be, Protestant or Catholic, before
instructing her ! And the Duke of Hanover
having heard all Gourville's proposal, said that a
change would be advantageous to his house, but
that he himself was too old to change.

This shrewd woman had such keen eyes that
she knew how to shut them upon occasion, and
was blind to many faults which it appeared that
her husband the Bishop of Osnaburg and Duke
of Hanover committed. He loved to take his
pleasure like other sovereigns — was a merry
prince, fond of dinner and the bottle ; liked to
go to Italy, as his brothers had done before him ;

and we read how he jovially sold 6,700 of his
Hanoverians to the seigniory of Venice. They
went bravely off to the Morea, under command
of Ernest's son, Prince Max, and only 1,400 of
them ever came home again. The German
princes sold a good deal of this kind of stock.
You may remember how George III.'s Government purchased Hessians, and the use we made
of them during the War of Independence.

The ducats Duke Ernest got for his soldiers he
spent in a series of the most brilliant entertain-
ments. Nevertheless, the jovial prince was eco-
nomical, and kept a steady eye upon his own
interests. He achieved the electoral dignity for
himself: he married his eldest son George to his
beautiful cousin of Zell; and sending his sons
out in command of armies to fight—now on this
side, now on that—he lived on, taking his pleasure, and scheming his schemes, a merry, wise
prince enough, not, I fear, a moral prince, of
which kind we shall have but very few specimens
in the course of these lectures.

Ernest Augustus had seven children in all,
some of whom were scapegraces, and rebelled
against the parental system of primogeniture and

non-division of property which the elector ordained. " Gustchen," the electress writes about
her second son :—" Poor Gus is thrust out, and
his father will give him no more keep. I laugh
in the day, and cry all night about it ; for I am a
fool with my children." Three of the six died
fighting against Turks, Tartars, Frenchmen.
One of them conspired, revolted, fled to Rome,
leaving an agent behind him, whose head was
taken off. The daughter, of whose early education we have made mention, was married to the
Elector of Brandenburg, and so her religion
settled finally on the Protestant side.

A niece of the Electress Sophia—who had been
made to change her religion, and marry the Duke
of Orleans, brother of the French King; a woman
whose honest heart was always with her friends
and dear old Deutschland, though her fat little
body was confined at Paris, or Marly, or Versailles
—has left us, in her enormous correspondence
(part of which has been printed in German and
French), recollections of the Electress, and of
George her son. Elizabeth Charlotte was at
Osnaburg when George was born (1660). She
narrowly escaped a whipping for being in the way

on that auspicious day. She seems not to have liked little George, nor George grown up; and represents him as odiously hard, cold, and silent. Silent he may have been : not a jolly prince like his father before him, but a prudent, quiet, selfish potentate, going his own way, managing his own affairs, and understanding his own interests remarkably well.

In his father's lifetime, and at the head of the Hanover forces of 8,000 or 10,000 men, George served the Emperor, on the Danube against Turks, at the siege of Vienna, in Italy, and on the Rhine. When he succeeded to the Electorate, he handled its affairs with great prudence and dexterity. He was very much liked by his people of Hanover. He did not show his feelings much, but he cried heartily on leaving them ; as they used for joy when he came back. He showed an uncommon prudence and coolness of behaviour when he came into his kingdom ; exhibiting no elation; reasonably doubtful whether he should not be turned out some day ; looking upon himself only as a lodger, and making the most of his brief tenure of St. James's and Hampton Court ; plundering, it is true, somewhat, and dividing amongst

his German followers; but what could be expected
of a sovereign who at home could sell his subjects
at so many ducats per head, and make no scruple
in so disposing of them? I fancy a considerable
shrewdness, prudence, and even moderation in
his ways. The German Protestant was a cheaper,
and better, and kinder king than the Catholic
Stuart in whose chair he sate, and so far loyal to
England, that he let England govern herself.

Having these lectures in view I made it my
business to visit that ugly cradle in which our
Georges were nursed. The old town of Hanover
must look still pretty much as in the time when
George Louis left it. The gardens and pavilions
of Herrenhausen are scarce changed since the day
when the stout old Electress Sophia fell down in
her last walk there, preceding but by a few weeks
to the tomb James II.'s daughter, whose death
made way for the Brunswick Stuarts in England.

The two first royal Georges, and their father,
Ernest Augustus, had quite royal notions regarding marriage; and Louis XIV. and Charles II.
scarce distinguished themselves more at Versailles
or St. James's, than these German sultans in
their little city on the banks of the Leine. You

may see at Herrenhausen the very rustic theatre
in which the Platens danced and performed
masques, and sang before the Elector and his
sons. There are the very fauns and dryads of
stone still glimmering through the branches, still
grinning and piping their ditties of no tone, as in
the days when painted nymphs hung garlands
round them; appeared under their leafy arcades
with gilt crooks, guiding rams with gilt horns;
descended from " machines" in the guise of
Diana or Minerva; and delivered immense allego-
rical compliments to the princes returned home
from the campaign.

That was a curious state of morals and politics
in Europe; a queer consequence of the triumph
of the monarchical principle. Feudalism was
beaten down. The nobility, in its quarrels with
the crown, had pretty well succumbed, and the
monarch was all in all. He became almost divine:
the proudest and most ancient gentry of the land
did menial service for him. Who should carry
Louis XIV.'s candle when he went to bed? what
prince of the blood should hold the king's
shirt when his Most Christian Majesty changed
that garment?—the French memoirs of the seven-

teenth century are full of such details and
squabbles. The tradition is not yet extinct in
Europe. Any of you who were present, as
myriads were, at that splendid pageant, the opening of our Crystal Palace in London, must have
seen two noble lords, great officers of the household, with ancient pedigrees, with embroidered
coats, and stars on their breasts and wands in
their hands, walking backwards for near the space
of a mile, while the royal procession made its
progress. Shall we wonder—shall we be angry
—shall we laugh at these old-world ceremonies?
View them as you will, according to your mood;
and with scorn or with respect, or with anger and
sorrow, as your temper leads you. Up goes
Gesler's hat upon the pole. Salute that symbol
of sovereignty with heartfelt awe; or with a sulky
shrug of acquiescence, or with a grinning
obeisance; or with a stout rebellious No—clap
your own beaver down on your pate, and refuse to
doff it, to that spangled velvet and flaunting
feather. I make no comment upon the spectators'
behaviour; all I say is, that Gesler's cap is still
up in the market-place of Europe, and not a few
folks are still kneeling to it.

Put clumsy, high Dutch statues in place of the marbles of Versailles: fancy Herrenhausen waterworks in place of those of Marly: spread the tables with Schweinskopf, Specksuppe, Leber kuchen, and the like delicacies, in place of the French *cuisine ;* and fancy Frau von Kielmansegge dancing with Count Kammerjunker Quirini, or singing French songs with the most awful German accent: imagine a coarse Versailles, and we háve a Hanover before us. " I am now got into the region of beauty," writes Mary Wortley, from Hanover in 1716; " all the women have literally rosy cheeks, snowy foreheads and necks, jet eyebrows, to which may generally be added coalblack hair. These perfections never leave them to the day of their death, and have a very fine effect by candle-light ; but I could wish they were handsome with a little variety. They resemble one another as Mrs. Salmon's Court of Great Britain, and are in as much danger of melting away by too nearly approaching the fire." The sly Mary Wortley saw this painted seraglio of the first George at Hanover, the year after his accession to the British throne. There were great doings and feasts there. Here Lady Mary saw

George II. too. " I can tell you, without flattery
or partiality," she says, " that our young prince
has all the accomplishments that it is possible to
have at his age, with an air of sprightliness and
understanding, and a something so very engaging
in his behaviour that needs not the advantage
of his rank to appear charming." I find elsewhere similar panegyrics upon Frederick Prince of
Wales, George II.'s son; and upon George III.,
of course, and upon George IV. in an eminent
degree. It was the rule to be dazzled by princes,
and people's eyes winked quite honestly at that
royal radiance.

The Electoral Court of Hanover was numerous
—pretty well paid, as times went; above all, paid
with a regularity which few other European courts
could boast of. Perhaps you will be amused to
know how the Electoral Court was composed.
There were the princes of the house in the first
class; in the second, the single field-marshal of
the army (the contingent was 18,000, Pöllnitz
says, and the Elector had other 14,000 troops in
his pay). Then follow, in due order, the autho-
rities civil and military, the working privy coun-
cillors, the generals of cavalry and infantry, in

the third class; the high chamberlain, high marshals of the court, high masters of the horse, the major-generals of cavalry and infantry, in the fourth class, down to the majors, the Hofjunkers or pages, the secretaries or assessors, of the tenth class, of whom all were noble.

We find the master of the horse had 1,090 thalers of pay; the high chamberlain, 2,000—a thaler being about three shillings of our money. There were two chamberlains, and one for the princess; five gentlemen of the chamber, and five gentlemen ushers; eleven pages and personages to educate these young noblemen—such as a governor, a preceptor, a fecht-meister, or fencing master, and a dancing ditto, this latter with a handsome salary of 400 thalers. There were three body and court physicians, with 800 and 500 thalers; a court barber, 600 thalers; a court organist; two musikanten; four French fiddlers; twelve trumpeters, and a bugler; so that there was plenty of music, profane and pious, in Hanover. There were ten chamber waiters, and twenty-four lacqueys in livery; a maître-d'hôtel, and attendants of the kitchen; a French cook; a body cook; ten cooks; six cooks'

assistants; two Braten masters, or masters of the
roast—(one fancies enormous spits turning slowly,
and the honest masters of the roast beladling the
dripping); a pastry baker; a pie baker; and
finally, three scullions, at the modest remunera-
tion of eleven thalers. In the sugar-chamber
there were four pastrycooks (for the ladies, no
doubt); seven officers in the wine and beer cel-
lars; four bread bakers; and five men in the
plate-room. There were 600 horses in the Serene
stables—no less than twenty teams of princely
carriage horses, eight to a team; sixteen coach-
men; fourteen postilions; nineteen ostlers;
thirteen helps, besides smiths, carriage-masters,
horse-doctors, and other attendants of the stable.
The female attendants were not so numerous:
I grieve to find but a dozen or fourteen of
them about the Electoral premises, and only two
washerwomen for all the Court. These function-
aries had not so much to do as in the present
age. I own to finding a pleasure in these small-
beer chronicles. I like to people the old world,
with its every-day figures and inhabitants—not so
much with heroes fighting immense battles and
inspiring repulsed battalions to engage; or states-

men locked up in darkling cabinets and medi-
tating ponderous laws or dire conspiracies—as
with people occupied with their every-day work
or pleasure : my lord and lady hunting in the
forest, or dancing in the Court, or bowing to
their serene highnesses as they pass in to dinner;
John Cook and his procession bringing the meal
from the kitchen; the jolly butlers bearing in
the flagons from the cellar; the stout coachman
driving the ponderous gilt waggon, with eight
cream-coloured horses in housings of scarlet
velvet and morocco leather; a postilion on the
leaders, and a pair or a half-dozen of running
footmen scudding along by the side of the vehicle,
with conical caps, long silver-headed maces, which
they poised as they ran, and splendid jackets
laced all over with silver and gold. I fancy the
citizens' wives and their daughters looking out
from the balconies; and the burghers over their
beer and mumm, rising up, cap in hand, as the
cavalcade passes through the town with torch-
bearers, trumpeters blowing their lusty cheeks
out, and squadrons of jack-booted lifeguards-
men, girt with shining cuirasses, and bestriding
thundering chargers, escorting his highness's

coach from Hanover to Herrenhausen; or halting, mayhap, at Madame Platen's country house of Monplaisir, which lies half-way between the summer palace and the Residenz.

In the good old times of which I am treating, whilst common men were driven off by herds, and sold to fight the emperor's enemies on the Danube, or to bayonet King Louis's troops of common men on the Rhine, noblemen passed from court to court, seeking service with one prince or the other, and naturally taking command of the ignoble vulgar of soldiery which battled and died almost without hope of promotion. Noble adventurers travelled from court to court in search of employment; not merely noble males, but noble females too; and if these latter were beauties, and obtained the favourable notice of princes, they stopped in the courts, became the favourites of their Serene or Royal Highnesses; and received great sums of money and splendid diamonds; and were promoted to be duchesses, marchionesses, and the like; and did not fall much in public esteem for the manner in which they won their advancement. In this way Mdlle. de Querouailles, a beautiful French

lady, came to London on a special mission of
Louis XIV., and was adopted by our grateful
country and sovereign, and figured as Duchess
of Portsmouth. In this way the beautiful Aurora
of Königsmarck travelling about found favour in
the eyes of Augustus of Saxony, and became
the mother of Marshal Saxe, who gave us a
beating at Fontenoy; and in this manner the
lovely sisters Elizabeth and Melusina of Meissen-
bach (who had actually been driven out of Paris,
whither they had travelled on a like errand, by
the wise jealousy of the female favourite there in
possession) journeyed to Hanover, and became
favourites of the serene house there reigning.

That beautiful Aurora von Königsmarck and
her brother are wonderful as types of bygone
manners, and strange illustrations of the morals
of old days. The Königsmarcks were descended
from an ancient noble family of Brandenburgh, a
branch of which passed into Sweden, where it
enriched itself and produced several mighty men
of valour.

The founder of the race was Hans Christof,
a famous warrior and plunderer of the thirty
years' war. One of Hans' sons, Otto, appeared

as ambassador at the court of Louis XIV., and had to make a Swedish speech at his reception before the Most Christian King. Otto was a famous dandy and warrior, but he forgot the speech, and what do you think he did? Far from being disconcerted, he recited a portion of the Swedish Catechism to His Most Christian Majesty and his court, not one of whom understood his lingo with the exception of his own suite, who had to keep their gravity as best they might.

Otto's nephew, Aurora's elder brother, Carl Johann of Königsmarck, a favourite of Charles II., a beauty, a dandy, a warrior, a rascal of more than ordinary mark, escaped but deserved being hanged in England, for the murder of Tom Thynne of Longleat. He had a little brother in London with him at this time :—as great a beauty, as great a dandy, as great a villain as his elder. This lad, Philip of Königsmarck, also was implicated in the affair; and perhaps it is a pity he ever brought his pretty neck out of it. He went over to Hanover, and was soon appointed colonel of a regiment of H. E. Highness's dragoons. In early life he had been page in the court of Celle;

and it was said that he and the pretty Princess Sophia Dorothea, who by this time was married to her cousin George the Electoral prince, had been in love with each other as children. Their loves were now to be renewed, not innocently, and to come to a fearful end.

A biography of the wife of George I., by Dr. Doran, has lately appeared, and I confess I am astounded at the verdict which that writer has delivered, and at his acquittal of this most unfortunate lady. That she had a cold selfish libertine of a husband no one can doubt; but that the bad husband had a bad wife is equally clear. She was married to her cousin for money or convenience, as all princesses were married. She was most beautiful, lively, witty, accomplished: his brutality outraged her: his silence and coldness chilled her: his cruelty insulted her. No wonder she did not love him. How could love be a part of the compact in such a marriage as that? With this unlucky heart to dispose of, the poor creature bestowed it on Philip of Königsmarck, than whom a greater scamp does not walk the history of the seventeenth century. A hundred and eighty years after the fellow was thrust

into his unknown grave, a Swedish professor
lights upon a box of letters in the University
Library at Upsala, written by Philip and Dorothea
to each other, and telling their miserable story.

The bewitching Königsmarck had conquered
two female hearts in Hanover. Besides the
Electoral prince's lovely young wife Sophia Dorothea, Philip had inspired a passion in a hideous
old court lady, the Countess of Platen. The
princess seems to have pursued him with the
fidelity of many years. Heaps of letters followed
him on his campaigns, and were answered by the
daring adventurer. The princess wanted to fly
with him; to quit her odious husband at any
rate. She besought her parents to receive her
back; had a notion of taking refuge in France
and going over to the Catholic religion; had
absolutely packed her jewels for flight, and very
likely arranged its details with her lover, in that
last long night's interview, after which Philip
of Königsmarck was seen no more.

Königsmarck, inflamed with drink—there is
scarcely any vice of which, according to his own
showing, this gentleman was not a practitioner—
had boasted at a supper at Dresden of his

intimacy with the two Hanoverian ladies, not only with the princess, but with another lady powerful in Hanover. The Countess Platen, the old favourite of the Elector, hated the young Electoral Princess. The young lady had a lively wit, and constantly made fun of the old one. The princess's jokes were conveyed to the old Platen just as our idle words are carried about at this present day: and so they both hated each other.

The characters in the tragedy, of which the curtain was now about to fall, are about as dark a set as eye ever rested on. There is the jolly prince, shrewd, selfish, scheming, loving his cups and his ease (I think his good-humour makes the tragedy but darker); his princess, who speaks little but observes all; his old, painted Jezebel of a mistress; his son, the Electoral Prince, shrewd too, quiet, selfish, not ill-humoured, and generally silent, except when goaded into fury by the intolerable tongue of his lovely wife; there is poor Sophia Dorothea, with her coquetry and her wrongs, and her passionate attachment to her scamp of a lover, and her wild imprudences, and her mad artifices, and her insane fidelity, and her

3

furious jealousy regarding her husband (though she loathed and cheated him), and her prodigious falsehoods; and the confidante, of course, into whose hands the letters are slipped; and there is Lothario, finally, than whom, as I have said, one can't imagine a more handsome, wicked, worthless reprobate.

How that perverse fidelity of passion pursues the villain! How madly true the woman is, and how astoundingly she lies! She has bewitched two or three persons who have taken her up, and they won't believe in her wrong. Like Mary of Scotland, she finds adherents ready to conspire for her even in history, and people who have to deal with her are charmed, and fascinated, and bedevilled. How devotedly Miss Strickland has stood by Mary's innocence! Are there not scores of ladies in this audience who persist in it too? Innocent! I remember as a boy how a great party persisted in declaring Caroline of Brunswick was a martyred angel. So was Helen of Greece innocent. She never ran away with Paris, the dangerous young Trojan. Menelaus, her husband, illused her; and there never was any siege of Troy at all. So was Bluebeard's wife

innocent. She never peeped into the closet
where the other wives were with their heads off.
She never dropped the key, or stained it with
blood; and her brothers were quite right in finish-
ing Bluebeard, the cowardly brute! Yes, Caroline of Brunswick was innocent : and Madame
Laffarge never poisoned her husband ; and Mary
of Scotland never blew up hers ; and poor Sophia
Dorothea was never unfaithful ; and Eve never
took the apple—it was a cowardly fabrication of
the serpent's.

George Louis has been held up to execration as
a murderous Bluebeard, whereas the Electoral
Prince had no share in the transaction in which
Philip of Königsmarck was scuffled out of this
mortal scene. The prince was absent when the
catastrophe came. The princess had had a hundred warnings ; mild hints from her husband's
parents ; grim remonstrances from himself—but
took no more heed of this advice than such besotted poor wretches do. On the night of Sunday, the 1st of July, 1694, Königsmarck paid a
long visit to the princess, and left her to get ready
for flight. Her husband was away at Berlin ; her
carriages and horses were prepared and ready for

the elopement. Meanwhile, the spies of Countess
Platen had brought the news to their mistress.
She went to Ernest Augustus, and procured from
the Elector an order for the arrest of the Swede.
On the way by which he was to come, four guards
were commissioned to take him. He strove to
cut his way through the four men, and wounded
more than one of them. They fell upon him;
cut him down; and, as he was lying wounded on
the ground, the countess, his enemy, whom he
had betrayed and insulted, came out and beheld
him prostrate. He cursed her with his dying lips,
and the furious woman stamped upon his mouth
with her heel. He was despatched presently; his
body burnt the next day; and all traces of the
man disappeared. The guards who killed him
were enjoined silence under severe penalties. The
princess was reported to be ill in her apartments,
from which she was taken in October of the same
year, being then eight-and-twenty years old, and
consigned to the castle of Ahlden, where she
remained a prisoner for no less than thirty-two
years. A separation had been pronounced previously between her and her husband. She was
called henceforth the "Princess of Ahlden,"

and her silent husband no more uttered her
name.

Four years after the Königsmarck catastrophe,
Ernest Augustus, the first Elector of Hanover,
died, and George Louis, his son, reigned in his
stead. Sixteen years he reigned in Hanover,
after which he became, as we know, King of
Great Britain, France, and Ireland, Defender of
the Faith. The wicked old Countess Platen died
in the year 1706. She had lost her sight, but
nevertheless the legend says that she constantly
saw Königsmarck's ghost by her wicked old bed.
And so there was an end of her.

In the year 1700, the little Duke of Gloucester,
the last of poor Queen Anne's children, died, and
the folks of Hanover straightway became of prodigious importance in England. The Electress
Sophia was declared the next in succession to the
English throne. George Louis was created Duke
of Cambridge; grand deputations were sent over
from our country to Deutschland; but Queen
Anne, whose weak heart hankered after her
relatives at St. Germains, never could be got to
allow her cousin, the Elector Duke of Cambridge,
to come and pay his respects to her Majesty, and

take his seat in her House of Peers. Had the
queen lasted a month longer; had the English
Tories been as bold and resolute as they were
clever and crafty; had the prince whom the
nation loved and pitied been equal to his fortune, George Louis had never talked German in
St. James's Chapel Royal.

When the crown did come to George Louis he
was in no hurry about putting it on. He waited
at home for awhile; took an affecting farewell of
his dear Hanover and Herrenhausen; and set out
in the most leisurely manner to ascend " the
throne of his ancestors," as he called it in his
first speech to Parliament. He brought with him
a compact body of Germans, whose society he
loved, and whom he kept round the royal person.
He had his faithful German chamberlains; his
German secretaries; his negroes, captives of his
bow and spear in Turkish wars; his two ugly,
elderly German favourites, Mesdames of Kielmansegge and Schulenberg, whom he created
respectively Countess of Darlington and Duchess
of Kendal. The duchess was tall, and lean of
stature, and hence was irreverently nicknamed
the Maypole. The countess was a large-sized

noblewoman, and this elevated personage was denominated the Elephant. Both of these ladies loved Hanover and its delights; clung round the linden-trees of the great Herrenhausen avenue, and at first would not quit the place. Schulenberg, in fact, could not come on account of her debts; but finding the Maypole would not come, the Elephant packed up her trunk and slipped out of Hanover unwieldy as she was. On this the Maypole straightway put herself in motion, and followed her beloved George Louis. One seems to be speaking of Captain Macheath, and Polly, and Lucy. The king we had selected; the courtiers who came in his train; the English nobles who came to welcome him, and on many of whom the shrewd old cynic turned his back—I protest it is a wonderful satirical picture. I am a citizen waiting at Greenwich pier, say, and crying hurrah for King George; and yet I can scarcely keep my countenance, and help laughing at the enormous absurdity of this advent!

Here we are, all on our knees. Here is the Archbishop of Canterbury prostrating himself to the head of his church, with Kielmansegge and

Schulenberg with their ruddled cheeks grinning behind the defender of the faith. Here is my Lord Duke of Marlborough kneeling too, the greatest warrior of all times; he who betrayed King William—betrayed King James II.—betrayed Queen Anne—betrayed England to the French, the Elector to the Pretender, the Pretender to the Elector; and here are my Lords Oxford and Bolingbroke, the latter of whom has just tripped up the heels of the former; and if a month's more time had been allowed him, would have had King James at Westminster. The great Whig gentlemen made their bows and congées with proper decorum and ceremony; but yonder keen old schemer knows the value of their loyalty. " Loyalty," he must think, " as applied to me— it is absurd! There are fifty nearer heirs to the throne than I am. I am but an accident, and you fine Whig gentlemen take me for your own sake, not for mine. You Tories hate me; you archbishop, smirking on your knees, and prating about Heaven, you know I don't care a fig for your Thirty-nine Articles, and can't understand a word of your stupid sermons. You, my Lords Bolingbroke and Oxford—you know you were conspiring against me a month ago; and you, my Lord Duke of Marlborough—you would sell me or any man else, if you found your advantage in it. Come, my good Melusina, come, my honest Sophia, let us go into my private room, and have some oysters and some Rhine wine, and some pipes afterwards: let us make the best of our situation; let us take what we can get, and leave these bawling, brawling, lying English to shout, and fight, and cheat, in their own way!"

If Swift had not been committed to the statesmen of the losing side, what a fine satirical picture we might have had of that general *sauve qui peut* amongst the Tory party! How mum the Tories became; how the House of Lords and House of Commons chopped round; and how decorously the majorities welcomed King George!

Bolingbroke, making his last speech in the House of Lords, pointed out the shame of peerage, where several lords concurred to condemn in one general vote all that they had approved in former parliaments by many particular resolutions. And so their conduct was shameful. St. John had the best of the argument, but the worst of the vote. Bad times were come for him. He talked philo-

sophy, and professed innocence. He courted
retirement, and was ready to meet persecution ;
but, hearing that honest Mat Prior, who had been
recalled from Paris, was about to peach regarding
the past transactions, the philosopher bolted, and
took that magnificent head of his out of the ugly
reach of the axe.   Oxford, the lazy and good-
humoured, had more courage, and awaited the
storm at home.   He and Mat Prior both had
lodgings in the Tower, and both brought their
heads safe out of that dangerous menagerie.
When Atterbury was carried off to the same den
a few years afterwards, and it was asked, what
next should be done with him ?   " Done with
him ?   Fling him to the lions," Cadogan said,
Marlborough's lieutenant.   But the British lion
of those days did not care much for drinking the
blood of peaceful peers and poets, or crunching
the bones of bishops.   Only four men were
executed in London for the rebellion of 1715;
and twenty-two in Lancashire. Above a thousand
taken in arms, submitted to the king's mercy, and
petitioned to be transported to his majesty's
colonies in America.   I have heard that their
descendants took the loyalist side in the disputes

which arose sixty years after. It is pleasant to find that a friend of ours, worthy Dick Steele, was for letting off the rebels with their lives.

As one thinks of what might have been, how amusing the speculation is! We know how the doomed Scottish gentlemen came out at Lord Mar's summons, mounted the white cockade, that has been a flower of sad poetry ever since, and rallied round the ill-omened Stuart standard at Braemar. Mar, with 8,000 men, and but 1,500 opposed to him, might have driven the enemy over the Tweed, and taken possession of the whole of Scotland; but that the Pretender's duke did not venture to move when the day was his own. Edinburgh Castle might have been in King James's hands; but that the men who were to escalade it stayed to drink his health at the tavern, and arrived two hours too late at the rendezvous under the castle wall. There was sympathy enough in the town—the projected attack seems to have been known there—Lord Mahon quotes Sinclair's account of a gentleman not concerned, who told Sinclair, that he was in a house that evening where eighteen of them were drinking, as the facetious landlady said, "powdering their hair," for the attack of the castle. Suppose they had not stopped to powder their hair? Edinburgh Castle, and town, and all Scotland were King James's. The north of England rises, and marches over Barnet Heath upon London. Wyndham is up in Somersetshire; Packington in Worcestershire; and Vivian in Cornwall. The Elector of Hanover, and his hideous mistresses, pack up the plate, and perhaps the crown jewels in London, and are off *viá* Harwich and Helvoetsluys, for dear old Deutschland. The king—God save him!—lands at Dover, with tumultuous applause; shouting multitudes, roaring cannon, the Duke of Marlborough weeping tears of joy, and all the bishops kneeling in the mud. In a few years, mass is said in St. Paul's; matins and vespers are sung in York Minster; and Dr. Swift is turned out of his stall and deanery house at St. Patrick's, to give place to Father Dominic, from Salamanca. All these changes were possible then, and once thirty years afterwards—all this we might have had, but for the *pulveris exigui jactu*, that little toss of powder for the hair which the Scotch conspirators stopped to take at the tavern.

You understand the distinction I would draw between history—of which I do not aspire to be an expounder—and manners and life such as these sketches would describe. The rebellion breaks out in the north; its story is before you in a hundred volumes, in none more fairly than in the excellent narrative of Lord Mahon. The clans are up in Scotland; Derwentwater, Nithisdale and Forster are in arms in Northumberland —these are matters of history, for which you are referred to the due chroniclers. The Guards are set to watch the streets, and prevent the people wearing white roses. I read presently of a couple of soldiers almost flogged to death for wearing oakboughs in their hats on the 29th of May— another badge of the beloved Stuarts. It is with these we have to do, rather than the marches and battles of the armies to which the poor fellows belonged—with statesmen, and how they looked, and how they lived, rather than with measures of State, which belong to history alone. For example, at the close of the old queen's reign, it is known the Duke of Marlborough left the kingdom—after what menaces, after what prayers, lies, bribes offered, taken, refused, accepted; after

what dark doubling and tacking, let history, if
she can or dare, say. The queen dead; who so
eager to return as my lord duke? Who shouts
God save the king! so lustily as the great conqueror of Blenheim and Malplaquet? (By the
way, he will send over some more money for the
Pretender yet, on the sly.) Who lays his hand
on his blue ribbon, and lifts his eyes more gracefully to heaven than this hero? He makes a
quasi-triumphal entrance into London, by Temple
Bar, in his enormous gilt coach—and the enormous gilt coach breaks down somewhere by
Chancery Lane, and his highness is obliged to
get another. There it is we have him. We are
with the mob in the crowd, not with the great
folks in the procession. We are not the Historic
Muse, but her ladyship's attendant, tale-bearer—
valet de chambre—for whom no man is a hero;
and, as yonder one steps from his carriage to
the next handy conveyance, we take the number
of the hack; we look all over at his stars, rib-
bons, embroidery; we think within ourselves, O
you unfathomable schemer! O you warrior invincible! O you beautiful smiling Judas! What
master would you not kiss or betray? What

traitor's head, blackening on the spikes on yonder gate, ever hatched a tithe of the treason which has worked under your periwig ?

We have brought our Georges to London city, and if we would behold its aspect, may see it in Hogarth's lively perspective of Cheapside, or read of it in a hundred contemporary books which paint the manners of that age. Our dear old *Spectator* looks smiling upon the streets, with their innumerable signs, and describes them with his charming humour. " Our streets are filled with Blue Boars, Black Swans, and Red Lions, not to mention Flying Pigs and Hogs in Armour, with other creatures more extraordinary than any in the deserts of Africa." A few of these quaint old figures still remain in London town. You may still see there, and over its old hostel in Ludgate Hill, the Belle Sauvage to whom the *Spectator* so pleasantly alludes in that paper ; and who was, probably, no other than the sweet American Pocahontas, who rescued from death the daring Captain Smith. There is the Lion's Head, down whose jaws the *Spectator's* own letters were passed ; and over a great banker's in Fleet Street, the effigy of the wallet, which the founder of the

firm bore when he came into London a country
boy. People this street, so ornamented with
crowds of swinging chairmen, with servants bawling to clear the way, with Mr. Dean in his
cassock, his lacquey marching before him; or
Mrs. Dinah in her sack, tripping to chapel, her
footboy carrying her ladyship's great prayer-book;
with itinerant tradesmen, singing their hundred
cries (I remember fòrty years ago, as a boy in
London city, a score of cheery, familiar cries
that are silent now). Fancy the beaux thronging
to the chocolate-houses, tapping their snuff-boxes
as they issue thence, their periwigs appearing
over the red curtains. Fancy Saccharissa beckon-
ing and smiling from the upper windows, and a
crowd of soldiers brawling and bustling at the
door—gentlemen of the Life Guards, clad in
scarlet, with blue facings, and laced with gold at
the seams; gentlemen of the Horse Grenadiers,
in their caps of sky-blue cloth, with the garter
embroidered on the front in gold and silver;
men of the Halberdiers, in their long red coats,
as bluff Harry left them, with their ruffs and
velvet flat caps. Perhaps the king's majesty
himself is going to St. James's as we pass. If

he is going to parliament, he is in his coach-
and-eight, surrounded by his guards and the high
officers of his crown. Otherwise his majesty only
uses a chair, with six footmen walking before,
and six yeomen of the guard at the sides of the
sedan. The officers in waiting follow the king in
coaches. It must be rather slow work.

Our *Spectator* and *Tatler* are full of delightful
glimpses of the town life of those days. In the
company of that charming guide, we may go to
the opera, the comedy, the puppet show, the
auction, even the cockpit: we can take boat at
Temple Stairs, and accompany Sir Roger de
Coverley and Mr. Spectator to Spring Garden—
it will be called Vauxhall a few years since, when
Hogarth will paint for it. Would you not like to
step back into the past, and be introduced to
Mr. Addison?—not the Right Honourable Joseph
Addison, Esq., George I.'s Secretary of State,
but to the delightful painter of contemporary
manners; the man who, when in good-humour
himself, was the pleasantest companion in all
England. I should like to go into Lockit's with
him, and drink a bowl along with Sir R. Steele
(who has just been knighted by King George,

4

and who does not happen to have any money
to pay his share of the reckoning). I should
not care to follow Mr. Addison to his secretary's
office in Whitehall. There we get into politics.
Our business is pleasure, and the town, and the
coffee-house, and the theatre, and the Mall.
Delightful Spectator! kind friend of leisure hours!
happy companion! true Christian gentleman!
How much greater, better, you are than the king
Mr. Secretary kneels to!

You can have foreign testimony about old-
world London, if you like; and my before-quoted
friend, Charles Louis, Baron de Pöllnitz, will
conduct us to it. "A man of sense," says he,
"or a fine gentleman, is never at a loss for company in London, and this is the way the latter
passes his time. He rises late, puts on a frock,
and, leaving his sword at home, takes his cane,
and goes where he pleases. The park is com-
monly the place where he walks, because 'tis the
Exchange for men of quality. 'Tis the same
thing as the Tuileries at Paris, only the park has
a certain beauty of simplicity which cannot be
described. The grand walk is called the Mall;
is full of people at every hour of the day, but

especially at morning and evening, when their
Majesties often walk with the royal family, who
are attended only by a half-dozen yeomen of the
guard, and permit all persons to walk at the same
time with them. The ladies and gentlemen
always appear in rich dresses, for the English,
who, twenty years ago, did not wear gold lace
but in their army, are now embroidered and
bedaubed as much as the French. I speak of
persons of quality; for the citizen still contents
himself with a suit of fine cloth, a good hat and
wig, and fine linen. Everybody is well clothed
here, and even the beggars don't make so ragged
an appearance as they do elsewhere." After our
friend, the man of quality, has had his morning
or undress walk in the Mall, he goes home to
dress, and then saunters to some coffee-house or
chocolate-house frequented by the persons he
would see. "For 'tis a rule with the English
to go once a day at least to houses of this sort,
where they talk of business and news, read the
papers, and often look at one another without
opening their lips. And 'tis very well they are
so mute: for were they all as talkative as people
of other nations, the coffee-houses would be

intolerable, and there would be no hearing what one man said where they are so many. The chocolate-house in St. James's Street, where I go every morning to pass away the time, is always so full that a man can scarce turn about in it."

Delightful as London city was, King George I. liked to be out of it as much as ever he could; and when there, passed all his time with his Germans. It was with them as with Blucher, 100 years afterwards, when the bold old Reiter looked down from St. Paul's, and sighed out, "Was für Plunder!" The German women plundered; the German secretaries plundered; the German cooks and intendants plundered; even Mustapha and Mahomet, the German negroes, had a share of the booty. Take what you can get, was the old monarch's maxim. He was not a lofty monarch, certainly: he was not a patron of the fine arts: but he was not a hypocrite, he was not revengeful, he was not extravagant. Though a despot in Hanover, he was a moderate ruler in England. His aim was to leave it to itself as much as possible, and to live out of it as much as he could. His heart was in Hanover. When taken ill on his last journey, as he was

passing through Holland, he thrust his livid head
out of the coach-window, and gasped out, " Osnaburg, Osnaburg !"   He was more than fifty years
of age when he came amongst us : we took him
because we wanted him, because he served our
turn ; we laughed at his uncouth German ways,
and sneered at him.   He took our loyalty for
what it was worth ; laid hands on what money he
could ; kept us assuredly from Popery and wooden
shoes.   I, for one, would have been on his side
in those days.   Cynical, and selfish, as he was,
he was better than a king out of St. Germains
with the French king's orders in his pocket, and
a swarm of Jesuits in his train.

The Fates are supposed to interest themselves
about royal personages ; and so this one had
omens and prophecies specially regarding him.
He was said to be much disturbed at a prophecy
that he should die very soon after his wife ; and
sure enough, pallid Death, having seized upon
the luckless princess in her castle of Ahlden,
presently pounced upon H. M. King George I.,
in his travelling chariot, on the Hanover road.
What postilion can outride that pale horseman ?
It is said, George promised one of his left-handed

widows to come to her after death, if leave were
granted to him to revisit the glimpses of the
moon; and soon after his demise, a great raven
actually flying or hopping in at the Duchess of
Kendal's window at Twickenham, she chose to
imagine the king's spirit inhabited these plumes,
and took special care of her sable visitor. Affecting metempsychosis—funereal royal bird! How
pathetic is the idea of the duchess weeping over
it! When this chaste addition to our English
aristocracy died, all her jewels, her plate, her
plunder went over to her relations in Hanover.
I wonder whether her heirs took the bird, and
whether it is still flapping its wings over Herrenhausen?

The days are over in England of that strange
religion of king-worship, when priests flattered
princes in the Temple of God; when servility
was held to be ennobling duty; when beauty
and youth tried eagerly for royal favour; and
woman's shame was held to be no dishonour.
Mended morals and mended manners in courts
and people, are among the priceless consequences
of the freedom which George I. came to rescue
and secure. He kept his compact with his

English subjects; and if he escaped no more
than other men and monarchs from the vices of
his age, at least we may thank him for preserving
and transmitting the liberties of ours. In our
free air, royal and humble homes have alike been
purified; and Truth, the birthright of high and
low among us, which quite fearlessly judges our
greatest personages, can only speak of them now
in words of respect and regard. There are stains
in the portrait of the first George, and traits in
it which none of us need admire; but, among the
nobler features are justice, courage, moderation—
and these we may recognize ere we turn the
picture to the wall.

II.—GEORGE THE SECOND.

Ave Cæsar.

GEORGE THE SECOND.

N the afternoon of the 14th of June, 1727, two horsemen m i g h t have been perceived galloping along the road from Chelsea to Richmond. The foremost, cased in the jackboots of the period, was a broad-faced, jolly-looking, and very corpulent cavalier; but, by the manner in which he urged his horse, you might see that he was a bold as well as a skilful rider. Indeed, no man loved sport better; and in the hunting-fields of Norfolk, no squire rode more boldly after the fox, or cheered Ringwood and Sweettips more lustily, than he who now thundered over the Richmond road.

He speedily reached Richmond Lodge, and asked to see the owner of the mansion. The mistress of the house and her ladies, to whom our friend was admitted, said he could not be introduced to the master, however pressing the business might be. The master was asleep after his dinner; he always slept after his dinner: and woe be to the person who interrupted him! Nevertheless, our stout friend of the jackboots put the affrighted ladies aside, opened the forbidden door of the bedroom, wherein upon the bed lay a little gentleman; and here the eager messenger knelt down in his jack-boots.

He on the bed started up, and with many oaths and a strong German accent asked who was there, and who dared to disturb him?

"I am Sir Robert Walpole," said the messenger. The awakened sleeper hated Sir Robert Walpole. "I have the honour to announce to your Majesty that your royal father, King

George I., died at Osnaburg, on Saturday last, the 10th inst."

"*Dat is one big lie!*" roared out his sacred Majesty King George II.: but Sir Robert Walpole stated the fact, and from that day until three and thirty years after, George, the second of the name, ruled over England.

How the king made away with his father's will under the astonished nose of the Archbishop of Canterbury; how he was a choleric little sovereign; how he shook his fist in the face of his father's courtiers; how he kicked his coat and wig about in his rages, and called everybody thief, liar, rascal, with whom he differed: you will read in all the history books; and how he speedily and shrewdly reconciled himself with the bold minister, whom he had hated during his father's life, and by whom he was served during fifteen years of his own with admirable prudence, fidelity, and success. But for Sir Robert Walpole, we should have had the Pretender back again. But for his obstinate love of peace, we should have had wars, which the nation was not strong enough nor united enough to endure. But for his resolute counsels and good-humoured resistance we might

have had German despots attempting a Hanoverian
regimen over us : we should have had revolt,
commotion, want, and tyrannous misrule, in place
of a quarter of a century of peace, freedom, and
material prosperity, such as the country never
enjoyed, until that corrupter of parliaments, that
dissolute tipsy cynic, that courageous lover of
peace and liberty, that great citizen, patriot, and
statesman governed it.   In religion he was little
better than a heathen ; cracked ribald jokes at
bigwigs and bishops, and laughed at High Church
and Low.   In private life the old pagan revelled
in the lowest pleasures : he passed his Sundays
tippling at Richmond ; and his holydays bawling
after dogs, or boozing at Houghton with boors
over beef and punch.   He cared for letters no
more than his master did : he judged human
nature so meanly that one is ashamed to have to
own that he was right, and that men could be
corrupted by means so base.   But, with his hire-
ling House of Commons, he defended liberty
for us ; with his incredulity he kept Church-
craft down.   There were parsons at Oxford
as doubledealing and dangerous as any priests
out of Rome, and he routed them both.   He

gave Englishmen no conquests, but he gave them peace, and ease, and freedom; the three per cents. nearly at par; and wheat at five and six and twenty shillings a quarter.

It was lucky for us that our first Georges were not more high-minded men; especially fortunate that they loved Hanover so much as to leave England to have her own way. Our chief troubles began when we got a king who gloried in the name of Briton, and, being born in the country, proposed to rule it. He was no more fit to govern England than his grandfather and great-grand-father, who did not try. It was righting itself during their occupation. The dangerous, noble old spirit of cavalier loyalty was dying out; the stately old English High Church was emptying itself: the questions dropping, which, on one side and the other;—the side of loyalty, prerogative, church, and king;—the side of right, truth, civil and religious freedom,—had set generations of brave men in arms. By the time when George III. came to the throne, the combat between loyalty and liberty was come to an end; and Charles Edward, old, tipsy, and childless, was dying in Italy.

Those who are curious about European Court history of the last age know the memoirs of the Margravine of Bayreuth, and what a Court was that of Berlin, where George II.'s cousins ruled sovereign. Frederick the Great's father knocked down his sons, daughters, officers of state; he kidnapped big men all Europe over to make grenadiers of; his feasts, his parades, his wine parties, his tobacco parties, are all described. Jonathan Wild the Great in language, pleasures, and behaviour, is scarcely more delicate than this German sovereign. Louis XV., his life, and reign, and doings, are told in a thousand French memoirs. Our George II., at least, was not a worse king than his neighbours. He claimed and took the royal exemption from doing right which sovereigns assumed. A dull little man of low tastes he appears to us in England; yet Hervey tells us that this choleric prince was a great sentimentalist, and that his letters—of which he wrote prodigious quantities—were quite dangerous in their powers of fascination. He kept his sentimentalities for his Germans and his queen. With us English, he never chose to be familiar. He has been accused of avarice, yet he did not give

much money, and did not leave much behind him.
He did not love the fine arts, but he did not pretend to love them. He was no more a hypocrite
about religion than his father. He judged men
by a low standard; yet, with such men as were
near him, was he wrong in judging as he did?
He readily detected lying and flattery, and liars
and flatterers were perforce his companions. Had
he been more of a dupe he might have been more
amiable. A dismal experience made him cynical.
No boon was it to him to be clearsighted, and see
only selfishness and flattery round about him.
What could Walpole tell him about his Lords and
Commons, but that they were all venal? Did
not his clergy, his courtiers, bring him the same
story? Dealing with men and women in his rude,
sceptical way, he comes to doubt about honour,
male and female, about patriotism, about religion.
" He is wild, but he fights like a man," George I.,
the taciturn, said of his son and successor.
Courage George II. certainly had. The Electoral
Prince, at the head of his father's contingent, had
approved himself a good and brave soldier under
Eugene and Marlborough. At Oudenarde he
specially distinguished himself. At Malplaquet

the other claimant to the English throne won but little honour. There was always a question about James's courage. Neither then in Flanders, nor afterwards in his own ancient kingdom of Scotland, did the luckless Pretender show much resolution. But dapper little George had a famous tough spirit of his own, and fought like a Trojan. He called out his brother of Prussia, with sword and pistol; and I wish, for the interest of romancers in general, that that famous duel could have taken place. The two sovereigns hated each other with all their might; their seconds were appointed; the place of meeting was settled; and the duel was only prevented by strong representations made to the two, of the European laughter which would have been caused by such a transaction.

Whenever we hear of dapper George at war, it is certain that he demeaned himself like a little man of valour. At Dettingen his horse ran away with him, and with difficulty was stopped from carrying him into the enemy's lines. The king, dismounting from the fiery quadruped, said bravely: " Now I know I shall not run away;" and placed himself at the head of the foot, drew his sword, brandishing it at the whole of the French army, and calling out to his own men to come on, in bad English, but with the most famous pluck and spirit. In '45, when the Pretender was at Derby, and many people began to look pale, the king never lost his courage—not he. " Pooh! don't talk to me that stuff!" he said, like a gallant little prince as he was, and never for one moment allowed his equanimity, or his business, or his pleasures, or his travels, to be disturbed. On public festivals he always appeared in the hat and coat he wore on the famous day of Oudenarde; and the people laughed, but kindly, at the odd old garment, for bravery never goes out of fashion.

In private life the prince showed himself a worthy descendant of his father. In this respect, so much has been said about the first George's manners, that we need not enter into a description of the son's German harem. In 1705 he married a princess remarkable for beauty, for cleverness, for learning, for good temper—one of the truest and fondest wives ever prince was blessed with, and who loved him and was faithful to him, and he, in his coarse fashion, loved her to the last.

It must be told to the honour of Caroline of
Anspach, that, at the time when German princes
thought no more of changing their religion than
you of altering your cap, she refused to give up
Protestantism for the other creed, although an
Archduke, afterwards to be an Emperor, was
offered to her for a bridegroom. Her Protestant
relations in Berlin were angry at her rebellious
spirit; it was they who tried to convert her (it is
droll to think that Frederick the Great, who had
no religion at all, was known for a long time in
England as the Protestant hero), and these good
Protestants set upon Caroline a certain Father
Urban, a very skilful Jesuit, and famous winner
of souls. But she routed the Jesuit; and she
refused Charles VI.; and she married the little
Electoral Prince of Hanover, whom she tended
with love, and with every manner of sacrifice,
with artful kindness, with tender flattery, with
entire self-devotion, thenceforward until her life's
end.

When George I. made his first visit to Hanover,
his son was appointed regent during the royal
absence. But this honour was never again conferred on the Prince of Wales; he and his father

fell out presently. On the occasion of the christening of his second son, a royal row took place, and the prince, shaking his fist in the Duke of Newcastle's face, called him a rogue, and provoked his august father. He and his wife were turned out of St. James's, and their princely children taken from them, by order of the royal head of the family. Father and mother wept piteously at parting from their little ones. The young ones sent some cherries, with their love, to papa and mamma ; the parents watered the fruit with tears. They had no tears thirty-five years afterwards, when Prince Frederick died—their eldest son, their heir, their enemy.

The king called his daughter-in-law " *cette diablesse madame la princesse.*" The frequenters of the latter's court were forbidden to appear at the king's : their royal highnesses going to Bath, we read how the courtiers followed them thither, and paid that homage in Somersetshire which was forbidden in London. That phrase of " *cette diablesse madame la princesse* " explains one cause of the wrath of her royal papa. She was a very clever woman : she had a keen sense of humour : she had a dreadful tongue : she turned into ridicule the antiquated sultan and his hideous harem. She wrote savage letters about him home to members of her family. So, driven out from the royal presence, the prince and princess set up for themselves in Leicester Fields, "where," says Walpole, " the most promising of the young gentlemen of the next party, and the prettiest and liveliest of the young ladies, formed the new court." Besides Leicester House, they had their lodge at Richmond, frequented by some of the pleasantest company of those days. There were the Herveys, and Chesterfield, and little Mr. Pope from Twickenham, and with him, sometimes, the savage Dean of St. Patrick's, and quite a bevy of young ladies, whose pretty faces smile on us out of history. There was Lepell, famous in ballad song; and the saucy, charming Mary Bellenden, who would have none of the Prince of Wales's fine compliments, who folded her arms across her breast, and bade H.R.H. keep off; and knocked his purse of guineas into his face, and told him she was tired of seeing him count them. He was not an august monarch, this Augustus. Walpole tells how, one night at the royal card-table, the playful princesses pulled a chair away from under Lady Deloraine, who, in revenge, pulled the king's from under him, so that his Majesty fell on the carpet. In whatever posture one sees this royal George, he is ludicrous somehow; even at Dettingen, where he fought so bravely, his figure is absurd—calling out in his broken English, and lunging with his rapier, like a fencing-master. In contemporary caricatures, George's son, "the Hero of Culloden," is also made an object of considerable fun, as witness the following picture of him defeated by the French (1757) at Hastenbeck:

I refrain to quote from Walpole regarding George—for those charming volumes are in the hands of all who love the gossip of the last century. Nothing can be more cheery than Horace's letters. Fiddles sing all through them : wax-lights, fine dresses, fine jokes, fine plate, fine equipages, glitter and sparkle there: never was such a brilliant, jigging, smirking Vanity Fair as that through which he leads us. Hervey, the next great authority, is a darker spirit. About him there is something frightful: a few years since his heirs opened the lid of the Ick-worth box; it was as if a Pompeii was opened to us—the last century dug up, with its temples and its games, its chariots, its public places—lupanaria. Wandering through that city of the dead, that dreadfully selfish time, through those godless intrigues and feasts, through those crowds, pushing, and eager, and struggling—rouged, and lying, and fawning—I have wanted some one to be friends with. I have said to friends conver-sant with that history, " Show me some good person about that Court; find me, among those selfish courtiers, those dissolute, gay people, some one being that I can love and regard. There is that strutting little sultan, George II.; there is that hunchbacked, beetle-browed Lord

Chesterfield; there is John Hervey, with his deadly smile, and ghastly, painted face—I hate them. There is Hoadly, cringing from one bishopric to another: yonder comes little Mr. Pope, from Twickenham, with his friend, the Irish dean, in his new cassock, bowing too, but with rage flashing from under his bushy eye brows, and scorn and hate quivering in his smile. Can you be fond of these? Of Pope I might: at least I might love his genius, his wit, his greatness, his sensibility—with a certain conviction that at some fancied slight, some sneer which he imagined, he would turn upon me and stab me. Can you trust the queen? She is not of our order: their very position makes kings and queens lonely. One inscrutable attachment that inscrutable woman has. To that she is faithful, through all trial, neglect, pain, and time. Save her husband, she really cares for no created being. She is good enough to her children, and even fond enough of them: but she would chop them all up into little pieces to please him. In her intercourse with all around her, she was perfectly kind, gracious, and natural: but friends may die, daughters may depart, she will be as perfectly kind and gracious to the next set. If the king wants her, she will smile upon him, be she ever so sad; and walk with him, be she ever so weary; and laugh at his brutal jokes, be she in ever so much pain of body or heart. Caroline's devotion to her husband is a prodigy to read of. What charm had the little man? What was there in those wonderful letters of thirty pages long, which he wrote to her when he was absent, and to his mistresses at Hanover, when he was in London with his wife? Why did Caroline, the most lovely and accomplished princess of Germany, take a little red-faced staring princeling for a husband, and refuse an emperor? Why, to her last hour, did she love him so? She killed herself because she loved him so. She had the gout, and would plunge her feet in cold water in order to walk with him. With the film of death over her eyes, writhing in intolerable pain, she yet had a livid smile and a gentle word for her master. You have read the wonderful history of that death-bed? How she bade him marry again, and the reply the old king blubbered out, "*Non, non: j'aurai des maitresses.*" There never was such a ghastly farce. I watch the astonishing

scene—I stand by that awful bedside, wondering
at the ways in which God has ordained the lives,
loves, rewards, successes, passions, actions, ends
of his creatures—and can't but laugh, in the
presence of death, and with the saddest heart.
In that often-quoted passage from Lord Hervey,
in which the queen's death-bed is described, the
grotesque horror of the details surpasses all
satire : the dreadful humour of the scene is more
terrible than Swift's blackest pages, or Fielding's
fiercest irony. The man who wrote the story
had something diabolical about him : the terrible
verses which Pope wrote respecting Hervey, in
one of his own moods of almost fiendish malignity, I fear are true. I am frightened as I look
back into the past, and fancy I behold that
ghastly, beautiful face ; as I think of the queen
writhing on her death-bed, and crying out,
" Pray !—pray ! "—of the royal old sinner by her
side, who kisses her dead lips with frantic grief,
and leaves her to sin more ;—of the bevy of
courtly clergymen, and the archbishop, whose
prayers she rejects, and who are obliged for propriety's sake to shuffle off the anxious inquiries
of the public, and vow that her Majesty quitted

this life " in a heavenly frame of mind." What
a life!—to what ends devoted! What a vanity
of vanities! It is a theme for another pulpit
than the lecturer's. For a pulpit?—I think the
part which pulpits play in the deaths of kings is
the most ghastly of all the ceremonial: the lying
eulogies, the blinking of disagreeable truths, the
sickening flatteries, the simulated grief, the falsehood and sycophancies—all uttered in the name
of Heaven in our State churches: these monstrous threnodies have been sung from time im-
memorial over kings and queens, good, bad,
wicked, licentious. The State parson must bring
out his commonplaces; his apparatus of rhetorical
black-hangings. Dead king or live king, the
clergyman must flatter him—announce his piety
whilst living, and when dead, perform the obse-
quies of " our most religious and gracious king."

I read that Lady Yarmouth (my most religious
and gracious king's favourite) sold a bishopric to
a clergyman for 5,000l. (She betted him 5,000l.
that he would not be made a bishop, and he lost,
and paid her.) Was he the only prelate of his
time led up by such hands for consecration? As
I peep into George II.'s St. James's, I see crowds

of cassocks rustling up the back-stairs of the ladies of the Court; stealthy clergy slipping purses into their laps; that godless old king yawning under his canopy in his Chapel Royal, as the chaplain before him is discoursing. Discoursing about what?—about righteousness and judgment? Whilst the chaplain is preaching, the king is chattering in German almost as loud as the preacher; so loud that the clergyman—it may be one Dr. Young, he who wrote *Night Thoughts*, and discoursed on the splendours of the stars, the glories of heaven, and utter vanities of this world—actually burst out crying in his pulpit because the defender of the faith and dispenser of bishoprics would not listen to him! No wonder that the clergy were corrupt and indifferent amidst this indifference and corruption. No wonder that sceptics multiplied and morals degenerated, so far as they depended on the influence of such a king. No wonder that Whitfield cried out in the wilderness, that Wesley quitted the insulted temple to pray on the hillside. I look with reverence on those men at that time. Which is the sublimer spectacle—the good John Wesley, surrounded by his congrega-

tion of miners at the pit's mouth, or the queen's
chaplains mumbling through their morning office
in their ante-room, under the picture of the great
Venus, with the door opened into the adjoining
chamber, where the queen is dressing, talking
scandal to Lord Hervey, or uttering sneers at
Lady Suffolk, who is kneeling with the basin at
her mistress's side ?   I say I am scared as I look
round at this society—at this king, at these
courtiers, at these politicians, at these bishops—
at this flaunting vice and levity. Whereabouts
in this Court is the honest man ? Where is the
pure person one may like ? The air stifles one
with its sickly perfumes. There are some old-
world follies and some absurd ceremonials about
our Court of the present day, which I laugh at,
but as an Englishman, contrasting it with the
past, shall I not acknowledge the change of to-
day ? As the mistress of St. James's passes me
now, I salute the sovereign, wise, moderate,
exemplary of life; the good mother; the good
wife ; the accomplished lady; the enlightened
friend of art; the tender sympathizer in her
people's glories and sorrows.

Of all the Court of George and Caroline, I find

no one but Lady Suffolk with whom it seems
pleasant and kindly to hold converse. Even the
misogynist Croker, who edited her letters, loves
her, and has that regard for her with which her
sweet graciousness seems to have inspired almost
all men and some women who came near her.
I have noted many little traits which go to prove
the charms of her character (it is not merely
because she is charming, but because she is characteristic, that I allude to her). She writes
delightfully sober letters. Addressing Mr. Gay
at Tunbridge (he was, you know, a poet, penni-
less and in disgrace), she says : "The place you
are in, has strangely filled your head with physicians and cures ; but, take my word for it, many
a fine lady has gone there to drink the waters
without being sick ; and many a man has com-
plained of the loss of his heart, who had it in his
own possession. I desire you will keep yours ;
for I shall not be very fond of a friend without
one, and I have a great mind you should be in
the number of mine."

When Lord Peterborough was seventy years
old, that indomitable youth addressed some
flaming love-, or rather gallantry-, letters to

Mrs. Howard—curious relics they are of the romantic manner of wooing sometimes in use in those days. It is not passion; it is not love; it is gallantry: a mixture of earnest and acting; high-flown compliments, profound bows, vows, sighs and ogles, in the manner of the Clelie romances, and Millamont and Doricourt in the comedy. There was a vast elaboration of ceremonies and etiquette, of raptures—a regulated form for kneeling and wooing which has quite passed out of our downright manners. Henrietta Howard accepted the noble old earl's philandering; answered the queer love-letters with due acknowledgment; made a profound curtsey to Peterborough's profound bow; and got John Gay to help her in the composition of her letters in reply to her old knight. He wrote her charming verses, in which there was truth as well as grace. " O wonderful creature!" he writes:—

" O wonderful creature, a woman of reason!
  Never grave out of pride, never gay out of season!
  When so easy to guess who this angel should be,
  Who would think Mrs. Howard ne'er dreamt it was she ?"

The great Mr. Pope also celebrated her in lines not less pleasant, and painted a portrait of

what must certainly have been a delightful
lady :—

> " I know a thing that's most uncommon—
>   Envy, be silent and attend !—
> I know a reasonable woman,
>   Handsome, yet witty, and a friend :

> " Not warp'd by passion, aw'd by rumour,
>   Not grave through pride, or gay through folly :
> An equal mixture of good-humour
>   And exquisite soft melancholy.

> " Has she no faults, then (Envy says), sir ?
>   Yes, she has one, I must aver—
> When all the world conspires to praise her,
>   The woman's deaf, and does not hear ! "

Even the women concurred in praising and
loving her. The Duchess of Queensberry bears
testimony to her amiable qualities, and writes to
her : " I tell you so and so, because you love
children, and to have children love you." The
beautiful, jolly Mary Bellenden, represented by
contemporaries as " the most perfect creature ever
known," writes very pleasantly to her " dear
Howard," her " dear Swiss," from the country,
whither Mary had retired after her marriage, and
when she gave up being a maid of honour.
" How do you do, Mrs. Howard ? " Mary breaks

out. "How do you do, Mrs. Howard? that is all I have to say. This afternoon I am taken with a fit of writing; but as to matter, I have nothing better to entertain you, than news of my farm. I therefore give you the following list of the stock of eatables that I am fatting for my private tooth. It is well known to the whole county of Kent, that I have four fat calves, two fat hogs, fit for killing, twelve promising black pigs, two young chickens, three fine geese, with thirteen eggs under each (several being duck-eggs, else the others do not come to maturity); all this, with rabbits, and pigeons, and carp in plenty, beef and mutton at reasonable rates. Now, Howard, if you have a mind to stick a knife into anything I have named, say so!"

A jolly set must they have been, those maids of honour. Pope introduces us to a whole bevy of them, in a pleasant letter. "I went," he says, "by water to Hampton Court, and met the Prince, with all his ladies, on horseback, coming from hunting. Mrs. Bellenden and Mrs. Lepell took me into protection, contrary to the laws against harbouring papists, and gave me a dinner, with something I liked better, an opportunity of

conversation with Mrs. Howard. We all agreed
that the life of a maid of honour was of all
things the most miserable, and wished that all
women who envied it had a specimen of it. To
eat Westphalia ham of a morning, ride over
hedges and ditches on borrowed hacks, come home
in the heat of the day with a fever, and (what
is worse a hundred times) with a red mark on
the forehead from an uneasy hat—all this may
qualify them to make excellent wives for hunters.
As soon as they wipe off the heat of the day,
they must simper an hour and catch cold in the
princess's apartment; from thence to dinner with
what appetite they may; and after that till midnight, work, walk, or think which way they
please. No lone house in Wales, with a moun-
tain and rookery, is more contemplative than
this Court. Miss Lepell walked with me three
or four hours by moonlight, and we met no
creature of any quality but the king, who gave
audience to the vice-chamberlain all alone under
the garden wall."

I fancy it was a merrier England, that of our
ancestors, than the island which we inhabit.
People high and low amused themselves very

6—2

much more. I have calculated the manner in
which statesmen and persons of condition passed
their time—and what with drinking, and dining,
and supping, and cards, wonder how they got
through their business at all. They played all
sorts of games, which, with the exception of
cricket and tennis, have quite gone out of our
manners now. In the old prints of St. James's
Park, you still see the marks along the walk, to
note the balls when the Court played at Mall.
Fancy Birdcage Walk now so laid out, and Lord
John and Lord Palmerston knocking balls up and
down the avenue! Most of those jolly sports
belong to the past, and the good old games of
England are only to be found in old novels, in
old ballads, or the columns of dingy old newspapers, which say how a main of cocks is to be
fought at Winchester between the Winchester
men and the Hampton men; or how the
Cornwall men and the Devon men are going
to hold a great wrestling match at Totnes, and
so on.

A hundred and twenty years ago there were
not only country towns in England, but people
who inhabited them. We were very much more

gregarious ; we were amused by very simple
pleasures. Every town had its fair, every village
its wake. The old poets have sung a hundred
jolly ditties about great cudgel-playings, famous
grinning through horse-collars, great maypole
meetings, and morris-dances. The girls used
to run races clad in very light attire ; and the
kind gentry and good parsons thought no shame
in looking on. Dancing bears went about the
country with pipe and tabor. Certain well-
known tunes were sung all over the land for
hundreds of years, and high and low rejoiced
in that simple music. Gentlemen who wished
to entertain their female friends constantly sent
for a band. When Beau Fielding, a mighty
fine gentleman, was courting the lady whom he
married, he treated her and her companion at
his lodgings to a supper from the tavern, and
after supper they sent out for a fiddler—three
of them. Fancy the three, in a great wainscoted
room, in Covent Garden or Soho, lighted by
two or three candles in silver sconces, some
grapes and a bottle of Florence wine on the
table, and the honest fiddler playing old tunes
in quaint old minor keys, as the Beau takes

out one lady after the other, and solemnly dances
with her!

The very great folks, young noblemen, with
their governors, and the like, went abroad and
made the great tour; the home satirists jeered
at the Frenchified and Italian ways which they
brought back; but the greater number of people
never left the country. The jolly squire often
had never been twenty miles from home. Those
who did go went to the baths, to Harrogate, or
Scarborough, or Bath, or Epsom. Old letters
are full of these places of pleasure. Gay writes
to us about the fiddlers at Tunbridge; of the
ladies having merry little private balls amongst
themselves; and the gentlemen entertaining them
by turns with tea and music. One of the young
beauties whom he met did not care for tea:
" We have a young lady here," he says, " that
is very particular in her desires. I have known
some young ladies, who, if ever they prayed,
would ask for some equipage or title, a husband
or matadores: but this lady, who is but seven-
teen, and has 30,000l. to her fortune, places all
her wishes on a pot of good ale. When her
friends, for the sake of her shape and com-

plexion, would dissuade her from it, she answers,
with the truest sincerity, that by the loss of
shape and complexion she could only lose a husband, whereas ale is her passion."

Every country town had its assembly-room—
mouldy old tenements, which we may still see in
deserted inn-yards, in decayed provincial cities,
out of which the great wen of London has sucked
all the life. York, at assize times, and through-
out the winter, harboured a large society of
northern gentry. Shrewsbury was celebrated for
its festivities. At Newmarket, I read of "a vast
deal of good company, besides rogues and blacklegs;" at Norwich, of two assemblies, with a
prodigious crowd in the hall, the rooms, and the
gallery. In Cheshire (it is a maid of honour of
Queen Caroline who writes, and who is longing
to be back at Hampton Court, and the fun there) I
peep into a country house, and see a very merry
party: "We meet in the work-room before nine,
eat and break a joke or two till twelve, then we
repair to our own chambers and make ourselves
ready, for it cannot be called dressing. At noon
the great bell fetches us into a parlour, adorned
with all sorts of fine arms, poisoned darts, several

pair of old boots and shoes worn by men of might, with the stirrups of King Charles I., taken from him at Edgehill,"—and there they have their dinner, after which comes dancing and supper.

As for Bath, all history went and bathed and drank there. George II. and his queen, Prince Frederick and his Court, scarce a character one can mention of the early last century, but was seen in that famous Pump-room where Beau Nash presided, and his picture hung between the busts of Newton and Pope :

> " This picture, placed these busts between,
>   Gives satire all its strength :
> Wisdom and Wit are little seen,
>   But Folly at full length."

I should like to have seen the Folly. It was a splendid, embroidered, beruffled, snuff-boxed, red-heeled, impertinent Folly, and knew how to make itself respected. I should like to have seen that noble old madcap Peterborough in his boots (he actually had the audacity to walk about Bath in boots !), with his blue ribbon and stars, and a cabbage under each arm, and a chicken in his hand, which he had been cheapening for his dinner. Chesterfield came there many a time and gambled for hundreds, and grinned through his gout. Mary Wortley was there, young and beautiful; and Mary Wortley, old, hideous, and snuffy. Miss Chudleigh came there, slipping away from one husband, and on the look-out for another. Walpole passed many a day there; sickly, supercilious, absurdly dandified, and affected; with a brilliant wit, a delightful sensibility; and for his friends, a most tender, generous, and faithful heart. And if you and I had been alive then, and strolling down Milsom Street—hush! we should have taken our hats off, as an awful, long, lean, gaunt figure, swathed in flannels, passed by in its chair, and a livid face looked out from the window—great fierce eyes staring from under a bushy, powdered wig, a terrible frown, a terrible Roman nose—and we whisper to one another, "There he is! There's the great commoner! There is Mr. Pitt!" As we walk away, the abbey bells are set a-ringing; and we meet our testy friend Toby Smollett, on the arm of James Quin the actor, who tells us that the bells ring for Mr. Bullock, an eminent cowkeeper from Tottenham, who has just arrived

to drink the waters; and Toby shakes his cane
at the door of Colonel Ringworm—the Creole
gentleman's lodgings next his own—where the
colonel's two negroes are practising on the French
horn.

When we try to recall social England, we must
fancy it playing at cards for many hours every
day. The custom is well nigh gone out among
us now, but fifty years ago was general, fifty
years before that almost universal, in the country.
"Gaming has become so much the fashion,"
writes Seymour, the author of the *Court Gamester*,
"that he who in company should be ignorant of
the games in vogue, would be reckoned low-bred,
and hardly fit for conversation." There were
cards everywhere. It was considered ill-bred to
read in company. "Books were not fit articles
for drawing-rooms," old ladies used to say.
People were jealous, as it were, and angry with
them. You will find in Hervey that George II.
was always furious at the sight of books; and
his queen, who loved reading, had to practise it in
secret in her closet. But cards were the resource
of all the world. Every night, for hours, kings
and queens of England sat down and handled

their majesties of spades and diamonds. In
European Courts, I believe the practice still
remains, not for gambling, but for pastime. Our
ancestors generally adopted it. "Books! prithee,
don't talk to me about books," said old Sarah
Marlborough. "The only books I know are men
and cards." "Dear old Sir Roger de Coverley
sent all his tenants a string of hogs' puddings
and a pack of cards at Christmas," says the
Spectator, wishing to depict a kind landlord. One
of the good old lady writers in whose letters I
have been dipping cries out, "Sure, cards have
kept us women from a great deal of scandal!"
Wise old Johnson regretted that he had not
learnt to play. "It is very useful in life," he
says; "it generates kindness, and consolidates
society." David Hume never went to bed without his whist. We have Walpole, in one of his
letters, in a transport of gratitude for the cards.
"I shall build an order to Pam," says he, in his
pleasant dandified way, "for the escape of my
charming Duchess of Grafton." The duchess
had been playing cards at Rome, when she ought
to have been at a cardinal's concert, where the
floor fell in, and all the monsignors were pre-

cipitated into the cellar. Even the Nonconformist
clergy looked not unkindly on the practice. "I
do not think," says one of them, "that honest
Martin Luther committed sin by playing at backgammon for an hour or two after dinner, in order
by unbending his mind to promote digestion."
As for the High Church parsons, they all played,
bishops and all. On Twelfth-day the Court used
to play in state. "This being Twelfth-day, his
Majesty, the Prince of Wales, and the Knights
Companions of the Garter, Thistle, and Bath,
appeared in the collars of their respective orders.
Their Majesties, the Prince of Wales, and three
eldest Princesses, went to the Chapel Royal, preceded by the heralds. The Duke of Manchester
carried the sword of State. The king and prince
made offering at the altar of gold, frankincense,
and myrrh, according to the annual custom. At
night their Majesties played at hazard with the
nobility, for the benefit of the groom-porter; and
'twas said the king won 600 guineas; the queen,
360; Princess Amelia, twenty; Princess Caroline,
ten; the Duke of Grafton and the Earl of Portmore, several thousands."

Let us glance at the same chronicle, which is

of the year 1731, and see how others of our fore-fathers were engaged.

" Cork, 15th January.—This day, one Tim Croneen was, for the murder and robbery of Mr. St. Leger and his wife, sentenced to be hanged two minutes, then his head to be cut off, and his body divided in four quarters, to be placed in four cross-ways. He was servant to Mr. St. Leger, and committed the murder with the privity of the servant-maid, who was sentenced to be burned; also of the gardener, whom he knocked on the head, to deprive him of his share of the booty."

" January 3.—A postboy was shot by an Irish gentleman on the road near Stone, in Stafford-shire, who died in two days, for which the gentle-man was imprisoned."

" A poor man was found hanging in a gentle-man's stables at Bungay, in Norfolk, by a person who cut him down, and running for assistance, left his penknife behind him. The poor man recovering, cut his throat with the knife; and a river being nigh, jumped into it; but company coming, he was dragged out alive, and was like to remain so."

" The Honourable Thomas Finch, brother to the Earl of Nottingham, is appointed ambassador at the Hague, in the room of the Earl of Chesterfield, who is on his return home."

" William Cowper, Esq., and the Rev. Mr. John Cowper, chaplain in ordinary to her Majesty, and rector of Great Berkhampstead, in the county of Hertford, are appointed clerks of the commissioners of bankruptcy."

" Charles Creagh, Esq., and — Macnamara, Esq., between whom an old grudge of three years had subsisted, which had occasioned their being bound over about fifty times for breaking the peace, meeting in company with Mr. Eyres, of Galloway, they discharged their pistols, and all three were killed on the spot — to the great joy of their peaceful neighbours, say the Irish papers."

" Wheat is 26s. to 28s., and barley 20s. to 22s. a quarter ; three per cents., 92 ; best loaf sugar, 9¼d. ; Bohea, 12s. to 14s. ; Pekoe, 18s., and Hyson, 35s. per pound."

" At Exon was celebrated with great magnificence the birthday of the son of Sir W. Courtney, Bart., at which more than 1,000 persons were present. A bullock was roasted whole; a butt of wine and several tuns of beer and cyder were given to the populace. At the same time Sir William delivered to his son, then of age, Powdram Castle, and a great estate."

"Charlesworth and Cox, two solicitors, convicted of forgery, stood on the pillory at the Royal Exchange. The first was severely handled by the populace, but the other was very much favoured, and protected by six or seven fellows who got on the pillory to protect him from the insults of the mob."

"A boy killed by falling upon iron spikes, from a lamp-post, which he climbed to see Mother Needham stand in the pillory."

"Mary Lynn was burned to ashes at the stake for being concerned in the murder of her mistress."

"Alexander Russell, the foot soldier, who was capitally convicted for a street robbery in January sessions, was reprieved for transportation; but having an estate fallen to him, obtained a free pardon."

"The Lord John Russell married to the Lady Diana Spencer, at Marlborough House. He has

a fortune of 30,000*l.* down, and is to have
100,000*l.* at the death of the Duchess Dowager
of Marlborough, his grandmother."

" March 1 being the anniversary of the queen's
birthday, when her Majesty entered the forty-
ninth year of her age, there was a splendid
appearance of nobility at St. James's. Her
Majesty was magnificently dressed, and wore a
flowered muslin head-edging, as did also her
Royal Highness. The Lord Portmore was said
to have had the richest dress, though an
Italian Count had twenty-four diamonds instead
of buttons."

New clothes on the birthday were the fashion
for all loyal people. Swift mentions the custom
several times. Walpole is constantly speaking of
it; laughing at the practice, but having the very
finest clothes from Paris, nevertheless. If the
king and queen were unpopular, there were very
few new clothes at the drawing-room. In a paper
in the *True Patriot*, No. 3, written to attack the
Pretender, the Scotch, French, and Popery, Fielding supposes the Scotch and the Pretender in
possession of London, and himself about to be
hanged for loyalty,—when, just as the rope is

round his neck, he says: " My little girl entered
my bed-chamber, and put an end to my dream by
pulling open my eyes, and telling me that the
tailor had just brought home my clothes for his
Majesty's birthday." In his *Temple Beau*, the
beau is dunned " for a birthday suit of velvet,
40*l*." Be sure that Mr. Harry Fielding was
dunned too.

The public days, no doubt, were splendid, but
the private Court life must have been awfully
wearisome. " I will not trouble you," writes
Hervey to Lady Sundon, " with any account of
our occupations at Hampton Court. No mill-
horse ever went in a more constant track, or a
more unchanging circle ; so that by the assistance
of an almanack for the day of the week, and a
watch for the hour of the day, you may inform
yourself fully, without any other intelligence but
your memory, of every transaction within the
verge of the Court. Walking, chaises, levées,
and audiences fill the morning. At night the
king plays at commerce and backgammon, and the
queen at quadrille, where poor Lady Charlotte
runs her usual nightly gauntlet, the queen pulling
her hood, and the Princess Royal rapping her

knuckles. The Duke of Grafton takes his nightly
opiate of lottery, and sleeps as usual between the
Princesses Amelia and Caroline. Lord Grantham
strolls from one room to another (as Dryden says),
like some discontented ghost that oft appears, and
is forbid to speak ; and stirs himself about as
people stir a fire, not with any design, but in
hopes to make it burn brisker. At last the
king gets up; the pool finishes; and everybody has their dismission. Their Majesties
retire to Lady Charlotte and my Lord Lifford ;
my Lord Grantham, to Lady Frances and
Mr. Clark : some to supper, some to bed ; and
thus the evening and the morning make the
day."

The king's fondness for Hanover occasioned all
sorts of rough jokes among his English subjects,
to whom *sauer-kraut* and sausages have ever been
ridiculous objects. When our present Prince
Consort came among us, the people bawled out
songs in the streets indicative of the absurdity of
Germany in general. The sausage-shops produced enormous sausages which we might suppose were the daily food and delight of German
princes. I remember the caricatures at the

marriage of Prince Leopold with the Princess Charlotte. The bridegroom was drawn in rags. George III.'s wife was called by the people a beggarly German duchess; the British idea being that all princes were beggarly except British princes. King George paid us back. He thought there were no manners out of Germany. Sarah Marlborough once coming to visit the princess, whilst her Royal Highness was whipping one of the roaring royal children, "Ah!" says George, who was standing by, "you have no good manners in England, because you are not properly brought up when you are young." He insisted that no English cooks could roast, no English coachman could drive: he actually questioned the superiority of our nobility, our horses, and our roast beef!

Whilst he was away from his beloved Hanover, every thing remained there exactly as in the prince's presence. There were 800 horses in the stables, there was all the apparatus of chamberlains, court-marshals, and equerries; and court assemblies were held every Saturday, where all the nobility of Hanover assembled at what I can't but think a fine and touching ceremony.

A large arm-chair was placed in the assembly-room, and on it the king's portrait. The nobility advanced, and made a bow to the arm-chair, and to the image which Nebuchadnezzar the king had set up; and spoke under their voices before the august picture, just as they would have done had the King Churfürst been present himself.

He was always going back to Hanover. In the year 1729, he went for two whole years, during which Caroline reigned for him in England, and he was not in the least missed by his British subjects. He went again in '35 and '36; and between the years 1740 and 1755 was no less than eight times on the Continent, which amusement he was obliged to give up at the outbreak of the Seven Years' War. Here every day's amusement was the same. " Our life is as uniform as that of a monastery," writes a courtier whom Vehse quotes. " Every morning at eleven, and every evening at six, we drive in the heat to Herrenhausen, through an enormous linden avenue; and twice a day cover our coats and coaches with dust. In the king's society there never is the least change. At table, and at cards, he sees always the same faces, and at the end of the game retires into his chamber. Twice a week there is a French theatre; the other days there is play in the gallery. In this way, were the king always to stop in Hanover, one could make a ten years' calendar of his proceedings; and settle beforehand what his time of business, meals, and pleasure would be."

The old pagan kept his promise to his dying wife. Lady Yarmouth was now in full favour, and treated with profound respect by the Hanover society, though it appears rather neglected in England when she came among us. In 1740, a couple of the king's daughters went to see him at Hanover; Anna, the Princess of Orange (about whom, and whose husband and marriage-day, Walpole and Hervey have left us the most ludicrous descriptions), and Maria of Hesse Cassel, with their respective lords. This made the Hanover court very brilliant. In honour of his high guests, the king gave several *fêtes*; among others, a magnificent masked ball, in the green theatre at Herrenhausen—the garden theatre, with linden and box for screen, and grass for a carpet, where the Platens had danced to George and his father

the late sultan. The stage and a great part of
the garden were illuminated with coloured lamps.
Almost the whole court appeared in white domi-
noes, "like," says the describer of the scene,
"like spirits in the Elysian fields. At night,
supper was served in the gallery with three great
tables, and the king was very merry. After
supper dancing was resumed, and I did not get
home till five o'clock by full daylight to Hanover.
Some days afterwards we had in the opera-house
at Hanover, a great assembly. The king appeared
in a Turkish dress; his turban was ornamented
with a magnificent agraffe of diamonds; the
Lady Yarmouth was dressed as a sultana; nobody
was more beautiful than the Princess of Hesse."
So, while poor Caroline was resting in her coffin,
dapper little George, with his red face and his
white eyebrows and goggle-eyes, at sixty years of
age, is dancing a pretty dance with Madame
Walmoden, and capering about dressed up like
a Turk! For twenty years more, that little old
Bajazet went on in this Turkish fashion, until
the fit came which choked the old man, when he
ordered the side of his coffin to be taken out,
as well as that of poor Caroline's who had pre-

ceded him, so that his sinful old bones and ashes
might mingle with those of the faithful creature.
O strutting Turkey-cock of Herrenhausen! O
naughty little Mahomet! in what Turkish para-
dise are you now, and where be your painted
houris? So Countess Yarmouth appeared as a
sultana, and his Majesty in a Turkish dress wore
an agraffe of diamonds, and was very merry, was
he? Friends! he was your fathers' king as well
as 'mine—let us drop a respectful tear over his
grave.

He said of his wife that he never knew a
woman who was worthy to buckle her shoe: he
would sit alone weeping before her portrait, and
when he had dried his eyes, he would go off to
his Walmoden and talk of her. On the 25th
day of October, 1760, he being then in the
seventy-seventh year of his age, and the thirty-
fourth of his reign, his page went to take him
his royal chocolate, and behold! the most religious and gracious king was lying dead on the
floor. They went and fetched Walmoden; but
Walmoden could not wake him. The sacred
Majesty was but a lifeless corpse. The king was
dead; God save the king! But, of course, poets

and clergymen decorously bewailed the late one.
Here are some artless verses, in which an English
divine deplored the famous departed hero, and
over which you may cry or you may laugh,
exactly as your humour suits :—

" While at his feet expiring Faction lay,
    No contest left but who should best obey ;
    Saw in his offspring all himself renewed ;
    The same fair path of glory still pursued ;
    Saw to young George Augusta's care impart
    Whate'er could raise and humanize the heart ;
    Blend all his grandsire's virtues with his own,
    And form their mingled radiance for the throne—
    No farther blessing could on earth be given—
    The next degree of happiness was—heaven ! "

If he had been good, if he had been just, if
he had been pure in life, and wise in council,
could the poet have said much more ? It was a
parson who came and wept over this grave, with
Walmoden sitting on it, and claimed heaven for
the poor old man slumbering below. Here was
one who had neither dignity, learning, morals,
nor wit—who tainted a great society by a bad
example ; who in youth, manhood, old age, was
gross, low, and sensual ; and Mr. Porteus, afterwards my Lord Bishop Porteus, says the earth

was not good enough for him, and that his only place was heaven! Bravo, Mr. Porteus! The divine who wept these tears over George the Second's memory wore George the Third's lawn. I don't know whether people still admire his poetry or his sermons.

III.—GEORGE THE THIRD.

GEORGE THE THIRD.

WE have to glance over sixty years in as many minutes. To read the mere catalogue of characters who figured during that long period, would occupy our allotted time, and we should have all text and no sermon. England has to undergo the revolt of the American colonies; to submit to defeat and separation; to shake under

the volcano of the French Revolution ; to grapple
and fight for the life with her gigantic enemy
Napoleon ; to gasp and rally after that tremendous
struggle.   The old society, with its courtly splendours, has to pass away ; generations of statesmen
to rise and disappear ; Pitt to follow Chatham to
the tomb ; the memory of Rodney and Wolfe to
be superseded by Nelson's and Wellington's glory;
the old poets who unite us to Queen Anne's time
to sink into their graves ; Johnson to die, and
Scott and Byron to arise ; Garrick to delight the
world with his dazzling dramatic genius, and
Kean to leap on the stage and take possession of
the astonished theatre. Steam has to be invented;
kings to be beheaded, banished, deposed, restored.
Napoleon to be but an episode, and George III.
is to be alive through all these varied changes, to
accompany his people through all these revolutions
of thought, government, society ; to survive out
of the old world into ours.

When I first saw England, she was in mourn-
ing for the young Princess Charlotte, the hope of
the empire. I came from India as a child, and
our ship touched at an island on the way home,
where my black servant took me a long walk over

rocks and hills until we reached a garden, where we saw a man walking. " That is he," said the black man : " that is Bonaparte ! He eats three sheep every day, and all the little children he can lay hands on !" There were people in the British dominions besides that poor Calcutta serving-man, with an equal horror of the Corsican ogre.

With the same childish attendant, I remember peeping through the colonnade at Carlton House, and seeing the abode of the great Prince Regent. I can see yet the Guards pacing before the gates of the place. The place ? What place ? The palace exists no more than the palace of Nebuchadnezzar. It is but a name now. Where be the sentries who used to salute as the Royal chariots drove in and out ? The chariots, with the kings inside, have driven to the realms of Pluto ; the tall Guards have marched into darkness, and the echoes of their drums are rolling in Hades. Where the palace once stood, a hundred little children are paddling up and down the steps to St. James's Park. A score of grave gentlemen are taking their tea at the Athenæum Club ; as many grisly warriors are garrisoning the United Service Club opposite. Pall Mall is the great

social Exchange of London now—the mart of
news, of politics, of scandal, of rumour—the English forum, so to speak, where men discuss the last
despatch from the Crimea, the last speech of Lord
Derby, the next move of Lord John. And, now
and then, to a few antiquarians, whose thoughts
are with the past rather than with the present, it
is a memorial of old times and old people, and
Pall Mall is our Palmyra. Look! About this
spot, Tom of Ten Thousand was killed by
Königsmarck's gang. In that great red house
Gainsborough lived, and Culloden Cumberland,
George III.'s uncle. Yonder is Sarah Marlborough's palace, just as it stood when that
termagant occupied it. At 25, Walter Scott used
to live; at the house, now No. 79, and occupied
by the Society for the Propagation of the Gospel
in Foreign Parts, resided Mrs. Eleanor Gwynn,
comedian. How often has Queen Caroline's chair
issued from under yonder arch! All the men of
the Georges have passed up and down the street.
It has seen Walpole's chariot and Chatham's
sedan; and Fox, Gibbon, Sheridan, on their way
to Brookes's; and stately William Pitt stalking
on the arm of Dundas; and Hanger and Tom

Sheridan reeling out of Raggett's; and Byron limping into Wattier's; and Swift striding out of Bury Street; and Mr. Addison and Dick Steele, both perhaps a little the better for liquor; and the Prince of Wales and the Duke of York clattering over the pavement; and Johnson counting the posts along the streets, after dawdling before Dodsley's window; and Horry Walpole hobbling into his carriage, with a gimcrack just bought out at Christie's; and George Selwyn sauntering into White's.

In the published letters to George Selwyn we get a mass of correspondence by no means so brilliant and witty as Walpole's, or so bitter and bright as Hervey's, but as interesting, and even more descriptive of the time, because the letters are the work of many hands. You hear more voices speaking, as it were, and more natural than Horace's dandified treble, and Sporus's malignant whisper. As one reads the Selwyn letters —as one looks at Reynolds's noble pictures illustrative of those magnificent times and voluptuous people—one almost hears the voice of the dead past; the laughter and the chorus; the toast called over the brimming cups; the shout at the

racecourse or the gaming-table; the merry joke
frankly spoken to the laughing fine lady. How
fine those ladies were, those ladies who heard
and spoke such coarse jokes; how grand those
gentlemen!

I fancy that peculiar product of the past, the **fine**
gentleman, has almost vanished off the face of the
earth, and is disappearing like the beaver or the
Red Indian. We can't have fine gentlemen any
more, because we can't have the society in which
they lived. The people will not obey: the parasites will not be **as** obsequious as formerly:
children do not go down on their knees to beg
their parents' blessing: chaplains do not say
grace and retire before the pudding: servants
do not say 'your honour' and 'your worship' at
every moment: tradesmen do not stand hat in
hand as the gentleman passes: authors do not
wait for hours in gentlemen's anterooms with a
fulsome dedication, for which they hope to get
five guineas from his lordship. In the days when
there were fine gentlemen, Mr. Secretary Pitt's
under-secretaries did not dare to sit down before
him; but Mr. Pitt, in his turn, went down on his
gouty knees to George II.; and when George III.

spoke a few kind words to him, Lord Chatham burst into tears of reverential joy and gratitude; so awful was the idea of the monarch, and so great the distinctions of rank. Fancy Lord John Russell or Lord Palmerston on their knees whilst the Sovereign was reading a despatch, or beginning to cry because Prince Albert said something civil!

At the accession of George III., the patricians were yet at the height of their good fortune. Society recognized their superiority, which they themselves pretty calmly took for granted. They inherited not only titles and estates, and seats in the House of Peers, but seats in the House of Commons. There were a multitude of Government places, and not merely these, but bribes of actual 500*l*. notes, which members of the House took not much shame in assuming. Fox went into Parliament at 20 : Pitt was just of age : his father not much older. It was the good time for Patricians. Small blame to them if they took and enjoyed, and over-enjoyed, the prizes of politics, the pleasures of social life.

In these letters to Selwyn, we are made acquainted with a whole society of these defunct

fine gentlemen : and can watch with a curious
interest a life, which the novel-writers of that
time, I think, have scarce touched upon. To
Smollett, to Fielding even, a lord was a lord : a
gorgeous being with a blue ribbon, a coroneted
chair, and an immense star on his bosom, to
whom commoners paid reverence. Richardson, a
man of humbler birth than either of the above
two, owned that he was ignorant regarding the
manners of the aristocracy, and besought Mrs.
Donnellan, a lady who had lived in the great
world, to examine a volume of Sir Charles
Grandison, and point out any errors which she
might see in this particular. Mrs. Donnellan found
so many faults, that Richardson changed colour ;
shut up the book ; and muttered that it were
best to throw it in the fire. Here, in Selwyn, we
have the real original men and women of fashion
of the early time of George III. We can follow
them to the new club at Almack's : we can travel
over Europe with them : we can accompany them
not only to the public places, but to their country-
houses and private society. Here is a whole
company of them ; wits and prodigals ; some
persevering in their bad ways ; some repentant,

but relapsing; beautiful ladies, parasites, humble
chaplains, led captains. Those fair creatures
whom we love in Reynolds's portraits, and who
still look out on us from his canvases with their
sweet calm faces and gracious smiles—those fine
gentlemen who did us the honour to govern us;
who inherited their boroughs; took their ease in
their patent places; and slipped Lord North's
bribes so elegantly under their ruffles—we make
acquaintance with a hundred of these fine folks,
hear their talk and laughter, read of their loves,
quarrels, intrigues, debts, duels, divorces; can
fancy them alive if we read the book long enough.
We can attend at Duke Hamilton's wedding, and
behold him marry his bride with the curtain-ring:
we can peep into her poor sister's death-bed: we
can see Charles Fox cursing over the cards, or
March bawling out the odds at Newmarket: we
can imagine Burgoyne tripping off from St.
James's Street to conquer the Americans, and
slinking back into the club somewhat crestfallen
after his beating: we can see the young king
dressing himself for the drawing-room and asking
ten thousand questions regarding all the gentlemen : we can have high life or low, the struggle

at the Opera to behold the Violetta or the Zamperini—the Macaronies and fine ladies in their chairs trooping to the masquerade or Madame Cornelys's—the crowd at Drury Lane to look at the body of Miss Ray, whom Parson Hackman has just pistolled—or we can peep into Newgate, where poor Mr. Rice the forger is waiting his fate and his supper. "You need not be particular about the sauce for his fowl," says one turnkey to another : "for you know he is to be hanged in the morning." "Yes," replies the second janitor, "but the chaplain sups with him, and he is a terrible fellow for melted butter."

Selwyn has a chaplain and parasite, one Dr. Warner, than whom Plautus, or Ben Jonson, or Hogarth, never painted a better character. In letter after letter he adds fresh strokes to the portrait of himself, and completes a portrait not a little curious to look at now that the man has passed away; all the foul pleasures and gambols in which he revelled, played out; all the rouged faces into which he leered, worms and skulls; all the fine gentlemen whose shoebuckles he kissed, laid in their coffins. This worthy clergyman takes care to tell us that he does not believe

in his religion, though, thank heaven, he is
not so great a rogue as a lawyer. He goes on
Mr. Selwyn's errands, any errands, and is proud,
he says, to be that gentleman's proveditor. He
waits upon the Duke of Queensberry—old Q.—
and exchanges pretty stories with that aristocrat.
He comes home " after a hard day's christening,"
as he says, and writes to his patron before sitting
down to whist and partridges for supper. He
revels in the thoughts of ox-cheek and burgundy—
he is a boisterous, uproarious parasite, licks his
master's shoes with explosions of laughter and
cunning smack and gusto, and likes the taste of
that blacking as much as the best claret in
old Q.'s cellar. He has Rabelais and Horace
at his greasy fingers' ends. He is inexpressibly
mean, curiously jolly; kindly and good-natured
in secret—a tender-hearted knave, not a venom-
ous lickspittle. Jesse says, that at his chapel in
Long Acre, "he attained a considerable popularity by the pleasing, manly, and eloquent style
of his delivery." Was infidelity endemic, and
corruption in the air? Around a young king,
himself of the most exemplary life and undoubted
piety, lived a court society as dissolute as our

country ever knew. George II.'s bad morals bore
their fruit in George III.'s early years; as I
believe that a knowledge of that good man's
example, his moderation, his frugal simplicity,
and God-fearing life, tended infinitely to improve
the morals of the country and purify the whole
nation.

After Warner, the most interesting of Selwyn's
correspondents is the Earl of Carlisle, grandfather of the amiable nobleman at present Viceroy in Ireland.   The grandfather, too, was Irish
Viceroy, having previously been treasurer of the
king's household; and, in 1778, the principal
commissioner for treating, consulting, and agree-
ing upon the means of quieting the divisions
subsisting in his Majesty's colonies, plantations,
and possessions in North America. You may
read his lordship's manifestoes in the *Royal New
York Gazette*. He returned to England, having
by no means quieted the colonies; and speedily
afterwards the *Royal New York Gazette* somehow
ceased to be published.

This good, clever, kind, highly-bred Lord
Carlisle was one of the English fine gentlemen
who was well-nigh ruined by the awful debauchery

and extravagance which prevailed in the great
English society of those days. Its dissoluteness
was awful: it had swarmed over Europe after
the Peace; it had danced, and raced, and gambled
in all the courts. It had made its bow at Versailles; it had run its horses on the plain of
Sablons, near Paris, and created the Anglo-mania
there : it had exported vast quantities of pictures
and marbles from Rome and Florence: it had
ruined itself by building great galleries and
palaces for the reception of the statues and
pictures : it had brought over singing-women and
dancing-women from all the operas of Europe,
on whom my lords lavished their thousands,
whilst they left their honest wives and honest
children languishing in the lonely, deserted splendours of the castle and park at home.

Besides the great London society of those days,
there was another unacknowledged world, extravagant beyond measure, tearing about in the
pursuit of pleasure; dancing, gambling, drinking,
singing; meeting the real society in the public
places (at Ranelaghs, Vauxhalls, and Ridottos,
about which our old novelists talk so constantly),
and outvying the real leaders of fashion, in

luxury, and splendour, and beauty. For instance, when the famous Miss Gunning visited Paris as Lady Coventry, where she expected that her beauty would meet with the applause which had followed her and her sister through England, it appears she was put to flight by an English lady still more lovely in the eyes of the Parisians. A certain Mrs. Pitt took a box at the opera opposite the countess; and was so much handsomer than her ladyship, that the parterre cried out that this was the real English angel, whereupon Lady Coventry quitted Paris in a huff. The poor thing died presently of consumption, accelerated, it was said, by the red and white paint with which she plastered those luckless charms of hers. (We must represent to ourselves all fashionable female Europe, at that time, as plastered with white, and raddled with red.) She left two daughters behind her, whom George Selwyn loved (he was curiously fond of little children), and who are described very drolly and pathetically in these letters, in their little nursery, where passionate little Lady Fanny, if she had not good cards, flung hers into Lady Mary's face; and where they sate conspiring how they should receive a new mother-in-law whom their papa presently brought home. They got on very well with their mother-in-law, who was very kind to them ; and they grew up, and they were married, and they were both divorced afterwards—poor little souls ! Poor painted mother, poor society, ghastly in its pleasures, its loves, its revelries !

As for my lord commissioner, we can afford to speak about him ; because, though he was a wild and weak commissioner at one time, though he hurt his estate, though he gambled and lost ten thousand pounds at a sitting—" five times more," says the unlucky gentleman, " than I ever lost before ;" though he swore he never would touch a card again ; and yet, strange to say, went back to the table and lost still more : yet he repented of his errors, sobered down, and became a worthy peer and a good country gentleman, and returned to the good wife and the good children whom he had always loved with the best part of his heart. He had married at one-and-twenty. He found himself, in the midst of a dissolute society, at the head of a great fortune. Forced into luxury, and obliged to be a great lord and a great idler, he yielded to some temptations, and paid for them a bitter penalty of manly remorse; from some others he fled wisely, and ended by conquering them nobly. But he always had the good wife and children in his mind, and they saved him. "I am very glad you did not come to me the morning I left London," he writes to G. Selwyn, as he is embarking for America. "I can only say, I never knew till that moment of parting, what grief was." There is no parting now, where they are. The faithful wife, the kind, generous gentleman, have left a noble race behind them: an inheritor of his name and titles, who is beloved as widely as he is known; a man most kind, accomplished, gentle, friendly, and pure; and female descendants occupying high stations and embellishing great names; some renowned for beauty, and all for spotless lives, and pious matronly virtues.

Another of Selwyn's correspondents is the Earl of March, afterwards Duke of Queensberry, whose life lasted into this century; and who certainly as earl or duke, young man or greybeard, was not an ornament to any possible society. The legends about old Q. are awful. In Selwyn, in Wraxall, and contemporary chronicles, the observer of human nature may follow him, drinking, gambling, intriguing to the end of his career; when the wrinkled, palsied, toothless old Don Juan died, as wicked and unrepentant as he had been at the hottest season of youth and passion. There is a house in Piccadilly, where they used to show a certain low window at which old Q. sat to his very last days, ogling through his senile glasses the women as they passed by.

There must have been a great deal of good about this lazy, sleepy George Selwyn, which, no doubt, is set to his present credit. "Your friendship," writes Carlisle to him, " is so different from anything I have ever met with or seen in the world, that when I recollect the extraordinary proofs of your kindness, it seems to me like a dream." "I have lost my oldest friend and acquaintance, G. Selwyn," writes Walpole to Miss Berry: "I really loved him, not only for his infinite wit, but for a thousand good qualities." I am glad, for my part, that such a lover of cakes and ale should have had a thousand good qualities—that he should have been friendly, generous, warm-hearted, trustworthy. "I rise at six," writes Carlisle to him, from Spa (a great resort of fashionable people in our ancestors' days), "play at cricket till dinner, and dance in the evening, till I can scarcely crawl to bed at eleven. There is a life for you! You get up at nine; play with Raton your dog till twelve, in your dressing-gown; then creep down to White's; are five hours at table; sleep till supper-time; and then make two wretches carry you in a sedan-chair, with three pints of claret in you, three miles for a shilling." Occasionally, instead of sleeping at White's, George went down and snoozed in the House of Commons by the side of Lord North. He represented Gloucester for many years, and had a borough of his own, Ludgershall, for which, when he was too lazy to contest Gloucester, he sat himself. "I have given directions for the election of Ludgershall to be of Lord Melbourne and myself," he writes to the Premier, whose friend he was, and who was himself as sleepy, as witty, and as good-natured as George.

If, in looking at the lives of princes, courtiers, men of rank and fashion, we must perforce depict them as idle, profligate, and criminal, we must make allowances for the rich men's failings, and

recollect that we, too, were very likely indolent
and voluptuous, had we no motive for work, a
mortal's natural taste for pleasure, and the daily
temptation of a large income. What could a great
peer, with a great castle and park, and a great
fortune, do but be splendid and idle? In these
letters of Lord Carlisle's from which I have been
quoting, there is many a just complaint made by
the kind-hearted young nobleman of the state
which he is obliged to keep; the magnificence in
which he must live; the idleness to which his
position as a peer of England bound him. Better
for him had he been a lawyer at his desk, or
a clerk in his office;—a thousand times better
chance for happiness, education, employment,
security from temptation. A few years since the
profession of arms was the only one which our
nobles could follow. The church, the bar, medi-
cine, literature, the arts, commerce, were below
them. It is to the middle class we must look
for the safety of England: the working educated
men, away from Lord North's bribery in the
senate; the good clergy not corrupted into parasites by hopes of preferment; the tradesmen
rising into manly opulence; the painters pursuing

their gentle calling; the men of letters in their
quiet studies; these are the men whom we love
and like to read of in the last age. How small
the grandees and the men of pleasure look
beside them! how contemptible the story of the
George III. court squabbles are beside the recorded
talk of dear old Johnson! What is the grandest
entertainment at Windsor, compared to a night
at the club over its modest cups, with Percy and
Langton, and Goldsmith, and poor Bozzy at the
table? I declare I think, of all the polite men
of that age, Joshua Reynolds was the finest
gentleman. And they were good, as well as
witty and wise, those dear old friends of the past.
Their minds were not debauched by excess, or
effeminate with luxury. They toiled their noble
day's labour: they rested, and took their kindly
pleasure: they cheered their holiday meetings
with generous wit and hearty interchange of
thought: they were no prudes, but no blush need
follow their conversation: they were merry, but
no riot came out of their cups. Ah! I would
have liked a night at the Turk's head, even
though bad news had arrived from the colonies,
and Doctor Johnson was growling against the

rebels; to have sat with him and Goldy; and to
have heard Burke, the finest talker in the world;
and to have had Garrick flashing in with a story
from his theatre!—I like, I say, to think of that
society; and not merely how pleasant and how
wise, but how *good* they were. I think it was on
going home one night from the club that Edmund
Burke—his noble soul full of great thoughts, be
sure, for they never left him; his heart full of
gentleness—was accosted by a poor wandering
woman, to whom he spoke words of kindness;
and moved by the tears of this Magdalen, perhaps having caused them by the good words he
spoke to her, he took her home to the house of
his wife and children, and never left her until he
had found the means of restoring her to honesty
and labour. O you fine gentlemen! you Marches,
and Selwyns, and Chesterfields, how small you
look by the side of these great men! Good-
natured Carlisle plays at cricket all day, and
dances in the evening "till he can scarcely
crawl," gaily contrasting his superior virtue with
George Selwyn's, "carried to bed by two wretches
at midnight with three pints of claret in him."
Do you remember the verses—the sacred verses

—which Johnson wrote on the death of his humble friend, Levett?

> " Well tried through many a varying year,
>   See Levett to the grave descend;
> Officious, innocent, sincere,
>   Of every friendless name the friend.

> " In misery's darkest cavern known,
>   His useful care was ever nigh,
> Where hopeless anguish poured the groan,
>   And lonely want retired to die.

> " No summons mocked by chill delay,
>   No petty gain disdained by pride,
> The modest wants of every day
>   The toil of every day supplied.

> " His virtues walked their narrow round,
>   Nor made a pause, nor left a void:
> And sure the Eternal Master found
>   His single talent well employed."

Whose name looks the brightest now, that of Queensberry the wealthy duke, or Selwyn the wit, or Levett the poor physician?

I hold old Johnson (and shall we not pardon James Boswell some errors for embalming him for us?) to be the great supporter of the British monarchy and church during the last age—better than whole benches of bishops, better than Pitts,

Norths, and the great Burke himself. Johnson
had the ear of the nation : his immense authority
reconciled it to loyalty, and shamed it out of
irreligion. When George III. talked with him,
and the people heard the great author's good
opinion of the sovereign, whole generations rallied
to the king. Johnson was revered as a sort of
oracle; and the oracle declared for church and
king. What a humanity the old man had! He
was a kindly partaker of all honest pleasures : a
fierce foe to all sin, but a gentle enemy to all
sinners. "What, boys, are you for a frolic?"
he cries, when Topham Beauclerc comes and
wakes him up at midnight: "I'm with you."
And away he goes, tumbles on his homely old
clothes, and trundles through Covent Garden
with the young fellows. When he used to fre-
quent Garrick's theatre, and had "the liberty of
the scenes," he says, "All the actresses knew
me, and dropped me a curtsey as they passed to
the stage." That would make a pretty picture :
it is a pretty picture in my mind, of youth, folly,
gaiety, tenderly surveyed by wisdom's merciful,
pure eyes.

George III. and his queen lived in a very

unpretending but elegant-looking house, on the
site of the hideous pile under which his
granddaughter at present reposes. The king's
mother inhabited Carlton House, which contemporary prints represent with a perfect para-
dise of a garden, with trim lawns, green arcades,
and vistas of classic statues. She admired these
in company with my Lord Bute, who had a fine
classic taste, and sometimes council took and
sometimes tea in the pleasant green arbours
along with that polite nobleman. Bute was
hated with a rage of which there have been
few examples in English history. He was the
butt for everybody's abuse; for Wilkes's devilish
mischief; for Churchill's slashing satire; for the
hooting of the mob that roasted the boot, his
emblem, in a thousand bonfires; that hated him
because he was a favourite and a Scotchman,
calling him "Mortimer," "Lothario," I know
not what names, and accusing his royal mistress
of all sorts of crimes—the grave, lean, demure,
elderly woman, who, I daresay, was quite as good
as her neighbours. Chatham lent the aid of his
great malice to influence the popular sentiment
against her. He assailed, in the House of Lords,

" the secret influence, more mighty than the
throne itself, which betrayed and clogged every
administration." The most furious pamphlets
echoed the cry. " Impeach the king's mother,"
was scribbled over every wall at the Court end of
the town, Walpole tells us. What had she done?
What had Frederick, Prince of Wales, George's
father, done, that he was so loathed by George II.
and never mentioned by George III.? Let us
not seek for stones to batter that forgotten grave,
but acquiesce in the contemporary epitaph over
him :—

> " Here lies Fred,
> Who was alive, and is dead.
> Had it been his father,
> I had much rather.
> Had it been his brother,
> Still better than another.
> Had it been his sister,
> No one would have missed her.
> Had it been the whole generation,
> Still better for the nation.
> But since 'tis only Fred,
> Who was alive, and is dead,
> There's no more to be said."

The widow with eight children round her,
prudently reconciled herself with the king, and
won the old man's confidence and good-will.

A shrewd, hard, domineering, narrow-minded woman, she educated her children according to her lights, and spoke of the eldest as a dull, good boy: she kept him very close: she held the tightest rein over him : she had curious prejudices and bigotries. His uncle, the burly Cumberland, taking down a sabre once, and drawing it to amuse the child—the boy started back and turned pale. The prince felt a generous shock: "What must they have told him about me ?" he asked.

His mother's bigotry and hatred he inherited with the courageous obstinacy of his own race; but he was a firm believer where his fathers had been free-thinkers, and a true and fond supporter of the Church, of which he was the titular defender. Like other dull men, the king was all his life suspicious of superior people. He did not like Fox; he did not like Reynolds; he did not like Nelson, Chatham, Burke; he was testy at the idea of all innovations, and suspicious of all innovators. He loved mediocrities; Benjamin West was his favourite painter; Beattie was his poet. The king lamented, not without pathos, in his after life, that his education had been

neglected. He was a dull lad brought up by
narrow-minded people. The cleverest tutors in
the world could have done little probably to
expand that small intellect, though they might
have improved his tastes, and taught his percep-
tions some generosity.

But he admired as well as he could. There is
little doubt that a letter, written by the little
Princess Charlotte of Mecklenburg Strelitz,—a
letter containing the most feeble commonplaces
about the horrors of war, and the most trivial
remarks on the blessings of peace, struck the
young monarch greatly, and decided him upon
selecting the young princess as the sharer of his
throne. I pass over the stories of his juvenile
loves—of Hannah Lightfoot, the Quaker, to
whom they say he was actually married (though
I don't know who has ever seen the register)—
of lovely black-haired Sarah Lennox, about whose
beauty Walpole has written in raptures, and who
used to lie in wait for the young prince, and
make hay at him on the lawn of Holland House.
He sighed and he longed, but he rode away from
her. Her picture still hangs in Holland House,
a magnificent master-piece of Reynolds, a canvas

worthy of Titian. She looks from the castle
window, holding a bird in her hand, at black-eyed
young Charles Fox, her nephew. The royal bird
flew away from lovely Sarah. She had to figure
as bridesmaid at her little Mecklenburg rival's
wedding, and died in our own time a quiet old
lady, who had become the mother of the heroic
Napiers.

They say the little princess who had written
the fine letter about the horrors of war—a beautiful letter without a single blot, for which she
was to be rewarded, like the heroine of the old
spelling-book story—was at play one day with
some of her young companions in the gardens of
Strelitz, and that the young ladies' conversation
was, strange to say, about husbands. " Who
will take such a poor little princess as me? "
Charlotte said to her friend, Ida von Bulow, and
at that very moment the postman's horn sounded,
and Ida said, " Princess! there is the sweet-
heart." As she said, so it actually turned out.
The postman brought letters from the splendid
young King of all England, who said, " Princess!
because you have written such a beautiful letter,
which does credit to your head and heart, come

and be Queen of Great Britain, France, and
Ireland, and the true wife of your most obedient
servant, George!" So she jumped for joy; and
went upstairs and packed all her little trunks;
and set off straightway for her kingdom in a
beautiful yacht, with a harpischord on board for
her to play upon, and around her a beautiful
fleet, all covered with flags and streamers, and
the distinguished Madame Auerbach complimented
her with an ode, a translation of which may be
read in the *Gentleman's Magazine* to the present
day :—

> " Her gallant navy through the main,
>   Now cleaves its liquid way.
> There to their queen a chosen train
>   Of nymphs due reverence pay.

> " Europa, when conveyed by Jove
>   To Crete's distinguished shore,
> Greater attention scarce could prove,
>   Or be respected more."

They met, and they were married, and for
years they led the happiest, simplest lives sure
ever led by married couple. It is said the king
winced when he first saw his homely little bride;
but, however that may be, he was a true and
faithful husband to her, as she was a faithful and

loving wife. They had the simplest pleasures—
the very mildest and simplest—little country
dances, to which a dozen couple were invited,
and where the honest king would stand up and
dance for three hours at a time to one tune;
after which delicious excitement they would go
to bed without any supper (the Court people
grumbling sadly at that absence of supper), **and**
get up quite early the next morning, and perhaps
the next night have another dance; or the queen
would play on the spinnet—she played pretty
well, Haydn said—or **the** king would read to her
a paper out of the *Spectator*, or perhaps one **of**
Ogden's sermons.   O Arcadia! what a life it
must **have** been!   There used to **be Sunday**
drawing-rooms at Court; but the young **king**
stopped these, as he stopped all that godless
gambling whereof we have made mention.   Not
that George was averse to any innocent pleasures,
or pleasures which he thought innocent.   He was
a patron of the arts, after his fashion; kind and
gracious to the artists whom he favoured, and
respectful to their calling.   He wanted once to
establish an **Order** of Minerva for literary and
scientific characters; the knights were to take

rank after the knights of the Bath, and to sport a straw-coloured ribbon and a star of sixteen points. But there was such a row amongst the *literati* as to the persons who should be appointed, that the plan was given up, and Minerva and her star never came down amongst us.

He objected to painting St. Paul's, as Popish practice; accordingly, the most clumsy heathen sculptures decorate that edifice at present. It is fortunate that the paintings, too, were spared, for painting and drawing were wofully unsound at the close of the last century; and it is far better for our eyes to contemplate whitewash (when we turn them away from the clergyman) than to look at Opie's pitchy canvases, or Fuseli's livid monsters.

And yet there is one day in the year—a day when old George loved with all his heart to attend it—when I think St. Paul's presents the noblest sight in the whole world: when five thousand charity children, with cheeks like nosegays, and sweet, fresh voices, sing the hymn which makes every heart thrill with praise and happiness. I have seen a hundred grand sights in the world—coronations, Parisian splendours,

Crystal Palace openings, Pope's chapels with their processions of long-tailed cardinals and quavering choirs of fat soprani—but think in all Christendom there is no such sight as Charity Children's Day. *Non Angli, sed angeli.* As one looks at that beautiful multitude of innocents: as the first note strikes : indeed one may almost fancy that cherubs are singing.

Of church music the king was always very fond, showing skill in it both as a critic and a performer. Many stories, mirthful and affecting, are told of his behaviour at the concerts which he ordered. When he was blind and ill he chose the music for the Ancient Concerts once, and the music and words which he selected were from *Samson Agonistes*, and all had reference to his blindness, his captivity, and his affliction. He would beat time with his music-roll as they sang the anthem in the Chapel Royal. If the page below was talkative or inattentive, down would come the music-roll on young scapegrace's powdered head. The theatre was always his delight. His bishops and clergy used to attend it, thinking it no shame to appear where that good man was seen. He is said not to have cared for Shakspeare or tragedy much; farces and pantomimes were his joy; and especially when clown swallowed a carrot or a string of sausages, he would laugh so outrageously that the lovely Princess by his side would have to say, " My gracious monarch, do compose yourself." But he continued to laugh, and at the very smallest farces, as long as his poor wits were left him.

There is something to me exceedingly touching in that simple early life of the king's. As long as his mother lived—a dozen years after his marriage with the little spinnet-player—he was a great, shy, awkward boy, under the tutelage of that hard parent. She must have been a clever, domineering, cruel woman. She kept her household lonely and in gloom, mistrusting almost all people who came about her children. Seeing the young Duke of Gloucester silent and unhappy once, she sharply asked him the cause of his silence. " I am thinking," said the poor child. " Thinking, sir! and of what ? " " I am thinking if ever I have a son I will not make him so unhappy as you make me." The other sons were all wild, except George. Dutifully every evening George and Charlotte paid their visit to the king's mother at Carlton House. She had a throat-complaint, of which she died; but to the last persisted in driving about the streets to show she was alive. The night before her death the resolute woman talked with her son and daughter-in-law as usual, went to bed, and was found dead there in the morning. "George, be a king!" were the words which she was for ever croaking in the ears of her son : and a king the simple, stubborn, affectionate, bigoted man tried to be.

He did his best ; he worked according to his lights ; what virtue he knew, he tried to practise ; what knowledge he could master, he strove to acquire. He was for ever drawing maps, for example, and learned geography with no small care and industry. He knew all about the family histories and genealogies of his gentry, and pretty histories he must have known. He knew the whole *Army List;* and all the facings, and the exact number of the buttons, and all the tags and laces, and the cut of all the cocked hats, pigtails, and gaiters in his army. He knew the *personnel* of the Universities; what doctors were inclined to Socinianism, and who were sound

Churchmen; he knew the etiquettes of his own and his grandfather's courts to a nicety, and the smallest particulars regarding the routine of ministers, secretaries, embassies, audiences; the humblest page in the ante-room, or the meanest helper in the stables or kitchen. These parts of the royal business he was capable of learning, and he learned. But, as one thinks of an office, almost divine, performed by any mortal man—of any single being pretending to control the thoughts, to direct the faith, to order the implicit obedience of brother millions, to compel them into war at his offence or quarrel; to command, "In this way you shall trade, in this way you shall think; these neighbours shall be your allies whom you shall help, these others your enemies whom you shall slay at my orders; in this way you shall worship God;"—who can wonder that, when such a man as George took such an office on himself, punishment and humiliation should fall upon people and chief?

Yet there is something grand about his courage. The battle of the king with his aristocracy remains yet to be told by the historian who shall view the reign of George more justly than the trumpery

panegyrists who wrote immediately after his
decease. It was he, with the people to back him,
who made the war with America; it was he and
the people who refused justice to the Roman
Catholics; and on both questions he beat the
patricians.   He bribed : he bullied : he darkly
dissembled on occasion : he exercised a slippery
perseverance, and a vindictive resolution, which
one almost admires as one thinks his character
over.   His courage was never to be beat.   It
trampled North under foot : it beat the stiff neck
of the younger Pitt : even his illness never conquered that indomitable spirit.   As soon as his
brain was clear, it resumed the scheme, only laid
aside when his reason left him : as soon as his
hands were out of the strait waistcoat, they took
up the pen and the plan which had engaged him
up to the moment of his malady.   I believe it is
by persons believing themselves in the right that
nine-tenths of the tyranny of this world has been
perpetrated. Arguing on that convenient premiss,
the Dey of Algiers would cut off twenty heads of a
morning ; Father Dominic would burn a score of
Jews in the presence of the most Catholic King,
and the Archbishops of Toledo and Salamanca

sing Amen. Protestants were roasted, Jesuits hung and quartered at Smithfield, and witches burned at Salem, and all by worthy people, who believed they had the best authority for their actions.

And so, with respect to old George, even Americans, whom he hated and who conquered him, may give him credit for having quite honest reasons for oppressing them. Appended to Lord Brougham's biographical sketch of Lord North are some autograph notes of the king, which let us most curiously into the state of his mind. "The times certainly require," says he, "the concurrence of all who wish to prevent anarchy. I have no wish but the prosperity of my own dominions, therefore I must look upon all who would not heartily assist me as bad men, as well as bad subjects." That is the way he reasoned. "I wish nothing but good, therefore every man who does not agree with me is a traitor and a scoundrel." Remember that he believed himself anointed by a Divine commission; remember that he was a man of slow parts and imperfect education; that the same awful will of Heaven which placed a crown upon

10

his head, which made him tender to his family, pure in his life, courageous and honest, made him dull of comprehension, obstinate of will, and at many times deprived him of reason. He was the father of his people; his rebellious children must be flogged into obedience. He was the defender of the Protestant faith; he would rather lay that stout head upon the block **than that** Catholics should have a share in the government of England. And you do not suppose that there are not honest bigots enough in all countries to back kings in this kind of statesmanship? Without doubt the American war was popular in England. In 1775 the address in favour of coercing the colonies was carried by 304 to 105 in the Commons, by **104** to 29 in the House of Lords. Popular?—so was the Revocation of the Edict of Nantes popular in France: so was the massacre **of** St. Bartholomew: so was the Inquisition exceedingly popular in Spain.

Wars and revolutions are, however, the politician's province. The great events of this long reign, the statesmen and orators who illustrated it, I do not pretend to make the subjects of an

hour's light talk.*   Let us return to our humbler
duty of court gossip. Yonder sits our little queen,
surrounded by many stout sons and fair daughters
whom she bore to her faithful George.   The his-   .
tory of the daughters, as little Miss Burney has

---

* Here are the figures, as drawn by young Gilray, of Lord
North, Mr. Fox, Mr. Pitt, and Mr. Burke.

painted them to us, is delightful.   They were
handsome—she calls them beautiful; they were
most kind, loving, and lady-like; they were
gracious to every person, high and low, who
served them.   They had many little accomplishments of their own.   This one drew: that one
played the piano: they all worked most pro-
digiously, and fitted up whole suits of rooms—
pretty, smiling Penelopes,—with their busy little
needles.   As we picture to ourselves the society

of eighty years ago, we must imagine hundreds
of thousands of groups of women in great high
caps, tight bodies, and full skirts, needling away,
whilst one of the number, or perhaps a favoured
gentleman in a pigtail, reads out a novel to the
company. Peep into the cottage at Olney, for
example, and see there Mrs. Unwin and Lady
Hesketh, those high-bred ladies, those sweet,
pious women, and William Cowper, that delicate
wit, that trembling pietist, that refined gentleman, absolutely reading out Jonathan Wild to
the ladies! What a change in our manners, in
our amusements, since then!

King George's household was a model of an
English gentleman's household. It was early;
it was kindly; it was charitable; it was frugal;
it was orderly; it must have been stupid to a
degree which I shudder now to contemplate. No
wonder all the princes ran away from the lap of
that dreary domestic virtue. It always rose,
rode, dined at stated intervals. Day after day
was the same. At the same hour at night the
king kissed his daughters' jolly cheeks; the
princesses kissed their mother's hand; and
Madame Thielke brought the royal nightcap.

At the same hour the equerries and women in waiting had their little dinner, and cackled over their tea. The king had his backgammon or his evening concert; the equerries yawned themselves to death in the anteroom; or the king and his family walked on Windsor slopes, the king holding his darling little princess Amelia by the hand; and the people crowded round quite good-naturedly; and the Eton boys thrust their chubby cheeks under the crowd's elbows; and the concert over, the king never failed to take his enormous cocked hat off, and salute his band, and say, "Thank you, gentlemen."

A quieter household, a more prosaic life than this of Kew or Windsor, cannot be imagined. Rain or shine, the king rode every day for hours; poked his red face into hundreds of cottages round about, and showed that shovel hat and Windsor uniform to farmers, to pig-boys, to old women making apple dumplings; to all sorts of people, gentle and simple, about whom countless stories are told. Nothing can be more undignified than these stories. When Haroun Alraschid visits a subject incog., the latter is sure to be very much the better for the caliph's magnificence. Old

George showed no such royal splendour. He used to give a guinea sometimes: sometimes feel in his pockets and find he had no money: often ask a man a hundred questions; about the number of his family, about his oats and beans, about the rent he paid for his house, and ride on. On one occasion he played the part of King Alfred, and turned a piece of meat with a string at a cottager's house. When the old woman came home, she found a paper with an enclosure of money, and a note written by the royal pencil: "Five guineas to buy a jack." It was not splendid, but it was kind and worthy of Farmer George. One day, when the king and queen were walking together, they met a little boy—they were always fond of children, the good folks—and patted the little white head. "Whose little boy are you?" asks the Windsor uniform. "I am the king's beef-eater's little boy," replied the child. On which the king said, "Then kneel down, and kiss the queen's hand." But the innocent offspring of the beefeater declined this treat. "No," said he, "I won't kneel, for if I do, I shall spoil my new breeches." The thrifty king ought to have hugged him and knighted him on the spot.

George's admirers wrote pages and pages of such
stories about him. One morning, before anybody
else was up, the king walked about Gloucester
town ; pushed over Molly the housemaid who was
scrubbing the doorsteps with her pail ; ran upstairs and woke all the equerries in their bed-
rooms ; and then trotted down to the bridge,
where, by this time, a dozen of louts were
assembled. " What! is this Gloucester New
Bridge?" asked our gracious monarch ; and the
people answered him, " Yes, your Majesty."
" Why, then, my boys," said he, " let us have a
huzzay!" After giving them which intellectual
gratification, he went home to breakfast. Our
fathers read these simple tales with fond pleasure;
laughed at these very small jokes ; liked the old
man who poked his nose into every cottage ; who
lived on plain wholesome roast and boiled ; who
despised your French kickshaws ; who was a true
hearty old English gentleman. You may have
seen Gilray's famous print of him—in the old
wig, in the stout old hideous Windsor uniform—
as the King of Brobdingnag, peering at a little
Gulliver, whom he holds up in his hand, whilst
in the other he has an opera-glass, through which

he surveys the pigmy? Our fathers chose to set up George as the type of a great king; and the little Gulliver was the great Napoleon. We prided ourselves on our prejudices; we blustered and bragged with absurd vain-glory; we dealt to our enemy a monstrous injustice of contempt and scorn; we fought him with all weapons, mean as well as heroic. There was no lie we would not believe; no charge of crime which our furious prejudice would not credit. I thought at one time of making a collection of the lies which the French had written against us, and we had published against them during the war: it would be a strange memorial of popular falsehood.

Their majesties were very sociable potentates: and the Court Chronicler tells of numerous visits which they paid to their subjects, gentle and simple: with whom they dined; at whose great country-houses they stopped; or at whose poorer lodgings they affably partook of tea and bread-and-butter. Some of the great folks spent enormous sums in entertaining their sovereigns. As marks of special favour, the king and queen sometimes stood as sponsors for the children of the nobility. We find Lady Salisbury was so honoured in the year 1786; and in the year 1802, Lady Chesterfield. The *Court News* relates how her ladyship received their majesties on a state bed " dressed with white satin and a profusion of lace: the counterpane of white satin embroidered with gold, and the bed of crimson satin lined with white." The child was first brought by the nurse to the Marchioness of Bath, who presided as chief nurse. Then the marchioness handed baby to the queen. Then the queen handed the little darling to the Bishop of Norwich, the officiating clergyman; and, the ceremony over, a cup of caudle was presented by the earl to his majesty on one knee, on a large gold waiter, placed on a crimson velvet cushion. Misfortunes would occur in these interesting genuflectory ceremonies of royal worship. Bubb Dodington, Lord Melcombe, a very fat, puffy man, in a most gorgeous court-suit, had to kneel, Cumberland says, and was so fat and so tight that he could not get up again. " Kneel, sir, kneel!" cried my lord in waiting to a country mayor who had to read an address, but who went on with his compliment standing. " Kneel, sir, kneel!" cries my lord, in dreadful alarm. " I can't!" says the mayor, turning

round; " don't you see I have got a wooden leg?"
In the capital *Burney Diary and Letters*, the home
and court life of good old King George and good
old Queen Charlotte are presented at portentous
length. The king rose every morning at six : and
had two hours to himself. He thought it effeminate to have a carpet in his bedroom. Shortly
before eight, the queen and the royal family were
always ready for him, and they proceeded to the
king's chapel in the castle. There were no fires
in the passages: the chapel was scarcely alight ;
princesses, governesses, equerries grumbled and
caught cold: but cold or hot, it was their duty to
go : and, wet or dry, light or dark, the stout old
George was always in his place to say amen to the
chaplain.

The queen's character is represented in *Burney*
at full length. She was a sensible, most decorous
woman ; a very grand lady on state occasions,
simple enough in ordinary life; well read as times
went, and giving shrewd opinions about books ;
stingy, but not unjust ; not generally unkind to
her dependants, but invincible in her notions of
etiquette, and quite angry if her people suffered
ill-health in her service. She gave Miss Burney

a shabby pittance, and led the poor young woman a life which well-nigh killed her. She never thought but that she was doing Burney the greatest favour, in taking her from freedom, fame, and competence, and killing her off with languor in that dreary court. It was not dreary to her. Had she been servant instead of mistress, her spirit would never have broken down : she never would have put a pin out of place, or been a moment from her duty. *She* was not weak, and she could not pardon those who were. She was perfectly correct in life, and she hated poor sinners with a rancour such as virtue sometimes has. She must have had awful private trials of her own : not merely with her children, but with her husband, in those long days about which nobody will ever know anything now; when he was not quite insane ; when his incessant tongue was babbling folly, rage, persecution; and she had to smile and be respectful and attentive under this intolerable ennui. The queen bore all her duties stoutly, as she expected others to bear them. At a State christening, the lady who held the infant was tired and looked unwell, and the Princess of Wales asked permission for her to sit down.

" Let her stand," said the queen, flicking the snuff off her sleeve. *She* would have stood, the resolute old woman, if she had had to hold the child till his beard was grown. " I am seventy years of age," the queen said, facing a mob of ruffians who stopped her sedan: " I have been fifty years queen of England, and I never was insulted before." Fearless, rigid, unforgiving little queen! I don't wonder that her sons revolted from her.

Of all the figures in that large family group which surrounds George and his queen, the prettiest, I think, is the father's darling, the Princess Amelia, pathetic for her beauty, her sweetness, her early death, and for the extreme passionate tenderness with which her father loved her. This was his favourite amongst all the children: of his sons, he loved the Duke of York best. Burney tells a sad story of the poor old man at Weymouth, and how eager he was to have this darling son with him. The king's house was not big enough to hold the prince; and his father had a portable house erected close to his own, and at huge pains, so that his dear Frederick should be near him. He clung on his arm all the

time of his visit : talked to no one else ; had
talked of no one else for some time before. The
prince, so long expected, stayed but a single
night. He had business in London the next day,
he said. The dulness of the old king's court
stupefied York and the other big sons of
George III. They scared equerries and ladies,
frightened the modest little circle, with their
coarse spirits and loud talk. Of little comfort,
indeed, were the king's sons to the king.

But the pretty Amelia was his darling ; and the
little maiden, prattling and smiling in the fond
arms of that old father, is a sweet image to look
on. There is a family picture in Burney, which
a man must be very hard-hearted not to like.
She describes an after-dinner walk of the royal
family at Windsor :—" It was really a mighty
pretty procession," she says. " The little
princess, just turned of three years old, in a robe-
coat covered with fine muslin, a dressed close cap,
white gloves, and fan, walked on alone and first,
highly delighted with the parade, and turning
from side to side to see everybody as she passed ;
for all the terracers stand up against the walls, to
make a clear passage for the royal family the

moment they come in sight. Then followed the king and queen, no less delighted with the joy of their little darling. The Princess Royal leaning on Lady Elizabeth Waldegrave, the Princess Augusta holding by the Duchess of Ancaster, the Princess Elizabeth led by Lady Charlotte Bertie, followed. Office here takes place of rank," says Burney,—to explain how it was that Lady E. Waldegrave, as lady of the bed-chamber, walked before a duchess ;—" General Bude, and the Duke of Montague, and Major Price as equerry, brought up the rear of the procession." One sees it ; the band playing its old music, the sun shining on the happy, loyal crowd ; and lighting the ancient battlements, the rich elms, and purple landscape, and bright greensward ; the royal standard drooping from the great tower yonder ; as old George passes, followed by his race, preceded by the charming infant, who caresses the crowd with her innocent smiles.

" On sight of Mrs. Delany, the king instantly stopped to speak to her; the queen, of course, and the little princess, and all the rest, stood still. They talked a good while with the sweet old lady, during which time the king once or twice addressed himself to me. I caught the queen's eye, and saw in it a little surprise, but by no means any displeasure, to see me of the party. The little princess went up to Mrs. Delany, of whom she is very fond, and behaved like a little angel to her. She then, with a look of inquiry and recollection, came behind Mrs. Delany to look at me. 'I am afraid,' said I, in a whisper, and stooping down, 'your Royal Highness does not remember me?' Her answer was an arch little smile, and a nearer approach, with her lips pouted out to kiss me."

The princess wrote verses herself, and there are some pretty plaintive lines attributed to her, which are more touching than better poetry :—

"Unthinking, idle, wild, and young,
I laughed, and danced, and talked, and sung:
And, proud of health, of freedom vain,
Dreamed not of sorrow, care, or pain;
Concluding, in those hours of glee,
That all the world was made for me.

"But when the hour of trial came,
When sickness shook this trembling frame,
When folly's gay pursuits were o'er,
And I could sing and dance no more,
It then occurred, how sad 'twould be
Were this world only made for me."

The poor soul quitted it—and ere yet she was
dead the agonized father was in such a state, that
the officers round about him were obliged to set
watchers over him, and from November, 1810,
George III. ceased to reign. All the world knows
the story of his malady : all history presents no
sadder figure than that of the old man, blind and
deprived of reason, wandering through the rooms
of his palace, addressing imaginary parliaments,
reviewing fancied troops, holding ghostly courts.
I have seen his picture as it was taken at this
time, hanging in the apartment of his daughter,
the Landgravine of Hesse Hombourg—amidst
books and Windsor furniture, and a hundred fond
reminiscences of her English home. The poor
old father is represented in a purple gown, his
snowy beard falling over his breast—the star
of his famous Order still idly shining on it. He
was not only sightless : he became utterly deaf.
All light, all reason, all sound of human voices,
all the pleasures of this world of God, were taken
from him. Some slight lucid moments he had ;
in one of which, the queen, desiring to see him,
entered the room, and found him singing a hymn,
and accompanying himself at the harpsichord.

11

When he had finished, he knelt down and prayed aloud for her, and then for his family, and then for the nation, concluding with a prayer for himself, that it might please God to avert his heavy calamity from him, but if not, to give him resignation to submit. He then burst into tears, and his reason again fled.

What preacher need moralize on this story; what words save the simplest are requisite to tell it? It is too terrible for tears. The thought of such a misery smites me down in submission before the Ruler of kings and men, the Monarch Supreme over empires and republics, the inscrutable Dispenser of life, death, happiness, victory. "O brothers," I said to those who heard me first in America—"O brothers! speaking the same dear mother tongue—O comrades! enemies no more, let us take a mournful hand together as we stand by this royal corpse, and call a truce to battle! Low he lies to whom the proudest used to kneel once, and who was cast lower than the poorest: dead, whom millions prayed for in vain. Driven off his throne; buffeted by rude hands; with his children in revolt; the darling of his old age killed before him untimely; our

Lear hangs over her breathless lips and cries,
' Cordelia, Cordelia, stay a little !'

> ' Vex not his ghost—oh ! let him pass—he hates him
> That would upon the rack of this tough world
> Stretch him out longer !'

Hush ! Strife and Quarrel, over the solemn grave !
Sound, trumpets, a mournful march. Fall, dark
curtain, upon his pageant, his pride, his grief, his
awful tragedy.

IV.—GEORGE THE FOURTH.

GEORGE THE FOURTH.

I N Twiss's amusing *Life of Eldon*, we read how, on the death of the Duke of York, the old chancellor became possessed of a lock of the defunct prince's hair; and so careful was he respecting the authenticity of the relic, that Bessy Eldon his wife

sate in the room with the young man from
Hamlet's, who distributed the ringlet into sepa-
rate lockets, which each of the Eldon family
afterwards wore. You know how, when George IV.
came to Edinburgh, a better man than he went
on board the royal yacht to welcome the king
to his kingdom of Scotland, seized a goblet from
which his majesty had just drunk, vowed it
should remain for ever as an heirloom in his
family, clapped the precious glass in his pocket,
and sate down on it and broke it when he got
home. Suppose the good sheriff's prize unbroken
now at Abbotsford, should we not smile with
something like pity as we beheld it? Suppose
one of those lockets of the no-Popery prince's
hair offered for sale at Christie's, *quot libras e
duce summo invenies?* how many pounds would you
find for the illustrious duke? Madame Tussaud
has got King George's coronation robes; is there
any man now alive who would kiss the hem of
that trumpery? He sleeps since thirty years:
do not any of you, who remember him, wonder
that you once respected and huzza'd and admired
him?

To make a portrait of him at first seemed a

matter of small difficulty. There is his coat,
his star, his wig, his countenance simpering under
it : with a slate and a piece of chalk, I could
at this very desk perform a recognizable likeness
of him. And yet after reading of him in scores
of volumes, hunting him through old magazines
and newspapers, having him here at a ball, there
at a public dinner, there at races and so forth, you
find you have nothing—nothing but a coat and wig
and a mask smiling below it—nothing but a great
simulacrum. His sire and grandsires were men.
One **knows** what they were like : what they
would do in given circumstances : that on
occasion they fought and demeaned themselves
like tough good soldiers. They had friends
whom they liked according to their natures ;
enemies whom they hated fiercely ; passions,
and actions, and individualities of their own.
The sailor king who came after George was a
man : the Duke of York was a man, big, burly,
loud, jolly, cursing, courageous. But this George,
what was he ? I look through all his life, and
recognize but a bow and a grin. I try and **take**
him to pieces, and find silk stockings, padding,
stays, a coat with frogs and a fur collar, a star

and blue ribbon, a pocket-handkerchief prodi-
giously scented, one of Truefitt's best nutty brown
wigs reeking with oil, a set of teeth and a huge
black stock, underwaistcoats, more underwaistcoats, and then nothing. I know of no sentiment
that he ever distinctly uttered. Documents are
published under his name, but people wrote them
—private letters, but people spelt them. He
put a great George P. or George R. at the
bottom of the page and fancied he had written
the paper: some bookseller's clerk, some poor
author, some *man* did the work; saw to the spell-
ing, cleaned up the slovenly sentences, and gave
the lax maudlin slipslop a sort of consistency.
He must have had an individuality: the dancing-
master whom he emulated, nay, surpassed—the
wig-maker who curled his toupee for him—the
tailor who cut his coats, had that. But, about
George, one can get at nothing actual. That
outside, I am certain, is pad and tailor's work;
there may be something behind, but what? We
cannot get at the character; no doubt never
shall. Will men of the future have nothing
better to do than to unswathe and interpret that
royal old mummy? I own I once used to think

it would be good sport to pursue him, fasten on him, and pull him down. But now I am ashamed to mount and lay good dogs on, to summon a full field, and then to hunt the poor game.

On the 12th August, 1762, the forty-seventh anniversary of the accession of the House of Brunswick to the English throne, all the bells in London pealed in gratulation, and announced that an heir to George III. was born. Five days afterwards the king was pleased to pass letters patent under the great seal, creating H. R. H. the Prince of Great Britain, Electoral Prince of Brunswick Lüneburg, Duke of Cornwall and Rothsay, Earl of Carrick, Baron of Renfrew, Lord of the Isles, and Great Steward of Scotland, Prince of Wales and Earl of Chester.

All the people at his birth thronged to see this lovely child ; and behind a gilt china-screen railing in St. James's Palace, in a cradle surmounted by the three princely ostrich feathers, the royal infant was laid to delight the eyes of the lieges. Among the earliest instances of homage paid to him, I read that " a curious Indian bow and arrows were sent to the prince from his father's faithful subjects in New York." He was

fond of playing with these toys: an old statesman, orator, and wit of his grandfather's and
great-grandfather's time, never tired of his
business, still eager in his old age to be well
at court, used to play with the little prince, and
pretend to fall down dead when the prince shot
at him with his toy bow and arrows—and get
up and fall down dead over and over again—to
the increased delight of the child. So that he
was flattered from his cradle upwards; and before
his little feet could walk, statesmen and courtiers
were busy kissing them.

There is a pretty picture of the royal infant—
a beautiful buxom child—asleep in his mother's
lap; who turns round and holds a finger to her
lip, as if she would bid the courtiers around
respect the baby's slumbers. From that day
until his decease, sixty-eight years after, I suppose
there were more pictures taken of that personage
than of any other human being who ever was
born and died—in every kind of uniform and
every possible court-dress—in long fair hair, with
powder, with and without a pig-tail—in every
conceivable cocked-hat—in dragoon uniform — in
Windsor uniform—in a field-marshal's clothes—

1780

1790.

The Regent.

The King.

in a Scotch kilt and tartans, with dirk and
claymore (a stupendous figure)—in a frogged
frock-coat with a fur collar and tight breeches
and silk stockings—in wigs of every colour, fair,
brown, and black—in his famous coronation robes
finally, with which performance he was so much
in love that he distributed copies of the picture
to all the courts and British embassies in Europe,
and to numberless clubs, town-halls, and private
friends. I remember as a young man how almost
every dining-room had his portrait.

There is plenty of biographical tattle about
the prince's boyhood. It is told with what
astonishing rapidity he learned all languages,
ancient and modern; how he rode beautifully,
sang charmingly, and played elegantly on the
violoncello. That he was beautiful was patent
to all eyes. He had a high spirit: and once,
when he had had a difference with his father,
burst into the royal closet and called out,
" Wilkes and liberty for ever!" He was so
clever, that he confounded his very governors
in learning; and one of them, Lord Bruce,
having made a false quantity in quoting Greek,
the admirable young prince instantly corrected

him. Lord Bruce could not remain a governor after this humiliation; resigned his office, and, to soothe his feelings, was actually promoted to be an earl! It is the most wonderful reason for promoting a man that ever I heard. Lord Bruce was made an earl for a blunder in prosody; and Nelson was made a baron for the victory of the Nile.

Lovers of long sums have added up the millions and millions which in the course of his brilliant existence this single prince consumed. Besides his income of 50,000*l.*, 70,000*l.*, 100,000*l.*, 120,000*l.* a-year, we read of three applications to parliament: debts to the amount of 160,000*l.*, of 650,000*l.*; besides mysterious foreign loans, whereof he pocketed the proceeds. What did he do for all this money? Why was he to have it? If he had been a manufacturing town, or a populous rural district, or an army of five thousand men, he would not have cost more. He, one solitary stout man, who did not toil, nor spin, nor fight,—what had any mortal done that he should be pampered so?

In 1784, when he was twenty-one years of age, Carlton Palace was given to him, and furnished

by the nation with as much luxury as could be
devised. His pockets were filled with money:
he said it was not enough; he flung it out of
window: he spent 10,000*l.* a-year for the coats
on his back. The nation gave him more money,
and more, and more. The sum is past counting.
He was a prince, most lovely to look on, and
christened Prince Florizel on his first appearance
in the world. That he was the handsomest prince
in the whole world was agreed by men, and alas!
by many women.

I suppose he must have been very graceful.
There are so many testimonies to the charm of
his manner, that we must allow him great elegance
and powers of fascination. He, and the King of
France's brother, the Count d'Artois, a charming
young prince who danced deliciously on the tight-
rope—a poor old tottering exiled king, who asked
hospitality of King George's successor, and lived
awhile in the palace of Mary Stuart—divided in
their youth the title of first gentleman of Europe.
We in England of course gave the prize to *our*
gentleman. Until George's death the propriety of
that award was scarce questioned or the doubters
voted rebels and traitors. Only the other day I was

reading in the reprint of the delightful *Noctes* of
Christopher North. The health of THE KING
is drunk in large capitals by the loyal Scotsman.
You would fancy him a hero, a sage, a statesman,
a pattern for kings and men. It was Walter
Scott who had that accident with the broken
glass I spoke of anon. He was the king's Scottish champion, rallied all Scotland to him, made
loyalty the fashion, and laid about him fiercely
with his claymore upon all the prince's enemies.
The Brunswicks had no such defenders as those
two Jacobite commoners, old Sam Johnson the
Lichfield chapman's son, and Walter Scott, the
Edinburgh lawyer's.

Nature and circumstance had done their utmost
to prepare the prince for being spoiled: the
dreadful dulness of papa's court, its stupid amusements, its dreary occupations, the maddening
humdrum, the stifling sobriety of its routine,
would have made a scapegrace of a much less
lively prince. All the big princes bolted from
that castle of *ennui* where old King George sat,
posting up his books and droning over his Handel;
and old Queen Charlotte over her snuff and her
tambour-frame. Most of the sturdy, gallant sons

settled down after sowing their wild oats, and became sober subjects of their father and brother —not ill liked by the nation, which pardons youthful irregularities readily enough, for the sake of pluck, and unaffectedness, and good-humour.

The boy is father of the man. Our prince signalized his entrance into the world by a feat worthy of his future life. He invented a new shoebuckle. It was an inch long and five inches broad. "It covered almost the whole instep, reaching down to the ground on either side of the foot." A sweet invention! lovely and useful as the prince on whose foot it sparkled. At his first appearance at a court ball, we read that "his coat was pink silk, with white cuffs; his waistcoat white silk, embroidered with various-coloured foil, and adorned with a profusion of French paste. And his hat was ornamented with two rows of steel beads, five thousand in number, with a button and loop of the same metal, and cocked in a new military style." What a Florizel! Do these details seem trivial? They are the grave incidents of his life. His biographers say that when he commenced housekeeping in that splendid new palace of his, the Prince of Wales had some windy projects of encouraging literature, science, and the arts; of having assemblies of literary characters; and societies for the encouragement of geography, astronomy, and botany. Astronomy, geography, and botany! Fiddlesticks! French ballet-dancers, French cooks, horse-jockeys, buffoons, procurers, tailors, boxers, fencing-masters, china, jewel, and gimcrack merchants—these were his real companions. At first he made a pretence of having Burke and Pitt and Sheridan for his friends. But how could such men be serious before such an empty scapegrace as this lad? Fox might talk dice with him, and Sheridan wine; but what else had these men of genius in common with their tawdry young host of Carlton House? That fribble the leader of such men as Fox and Burke! That man's opinions about the constitution, the India Bill, justice to the Catholics—about any question graver than the button for a waistcoat or the sauce for a partridge—worth anything! The friendship between the prince and the Whig chiefs was impossible. They were hypocrites in pretending to respect him, and if he broke the hollow compact between them, who shall blame him?

12—2

His natural companions were dandies and parasites. He could talk to a tailor or a cook; but, as the equal of great statesmen, to set up a creature, lazy, weak, indolent, besotted, of monstrous vanity, and levity incurable—it is absurd. They thought to use him, and did for awhile; but they must have known how timid he was; how entirely heartless and treacherous, and have expected his desertion. His next set of friends were mere table companions, of whom he grew tired too; then we hear of him with a very few select toadies, mere boys from school or the Guards, whose sprightliness tickled the fancy of the worn-out voluptuary. What matters what friends he had? He dropped all his friends; he never could have real friends. An heir to the throne has flatterers, adventurers who hang about him, ambitious men who use him; but friendship is denied him.

And women, I suppose, are as false and selfish in their dealings with such a character as men. Shall we take the Leporello part, flourish a catalogue of the conquests of this royal Don Juan, and tell the names of the favourites to whom, one after the other, George Prince flung his pocket-handkerchief? What purpose would it answer to say how Perdita was pursued, won, deserted, and by whom succeeded? What good in knowing that he did actually marry Mrs. Fitz-Herbert according to the rites of the Roman Catholic Church; that her marriage settlements have been seen in London; that the names of the witnesses to her marriage are known. This sort of vice that we are now come to presents no new or fleeting trait of manners. Debauchees, dissolute, heartless, fickle, cowardly, have been ever since the world began. This one had more temptations than most, and so much may be said in extenuation for him.

It was an unlucky thing for this doomed one, and tending to lead him yet farther on the road to the deuce, that, besides being lovely, so that women were fascinated by him; and heir apparent, so that all the world flattered him; he should have a beautiful voice, which led him directly in the way of drink: and thus all the pleasant devils were coaxing on poor Florizel; desire, and idleness, and vanity, and drunkenness, all clashing their merry cymbals and bidding him come on.

We first hear of his warbling sentimental ditties under the walls of Kew Palace by the moonlight banks of Thames, with Lord Viscount Leporello keeping watch lest the music should be disturbed.

Singing after dinner and supper was the universal fashion of the day. You may fancy all England sounding with choruses, some ribald, some harmless, but all occasioning the consumption of a prodigious deal of fermented liquor.

" The jolly muse her wings to try no frolic flights need take,
    But round the bowl would dip and fly, like swallows round a
        lake,"

sang Morris in one of his gallant Anacreontics, to which the prince many a time joined in chorus, and of which the burden is,—

" And that I think's a reason fair to drink and fill again."

This delightful boon companion of the prince's found " a reason fair" to forego filling and drinking, saw the error of his ways, gave up the bowl and chorus, and died retired and religious. The prince's table no doubt was a very tempting one. The wits came and did their utmost to amuse him. It is wonderful how the spirits rise, the wit brightens, the wine has an aroma, when a great man is at the head of the table. Scott, the loyal cavalier, the king's true liegeman, the very best *raconteur* of his time, poured out with an endless generosity his store of old-world learning, kindness, and humour. Grattan contributed to it his wondrous eloquence, fancy, feeling. Tom Moore perched upon it for awhile, and piped his most exquisite little love-tunes on it, flying away in a twitter of indignation afterwards, and attacking the prince with bill and claw. In such society, no wonder the sitting was long, and the butler tired of drawing corks. Remember what the usages of the time were, and that William Pitt, coming to the House of Commons after having drunk a bottle of port-wine at his own house, would go into Bellamy's with Dundas, and help finish a couple more.

You peruse volumes after volumes about our prince, and find some half-dozen stock stories—indeed not many more — common to all the histories. He was good-natured; an indolent, voluptuous prince, not unkindly. One story, the most favourable to him of all, perhaps, is that as Prince Regent he was eager to hear all that could

be said in behalf of prisoners condemned to death,
and anxious, if possible, to remit the capital sen-
tence. He was kind to his servants. There is a
story common to all the biographies, of Molly the
housemaid, who, when his household was to be
broken up, owing to some reforms which he tried
absurdly to practise, was discovered crying as she
dusted the chairs because she was to leave a
master who had a kind word for all his servants.
Another tale is that of a groom of the prince's
being discovered in corn and oat peculations, and
dismissed by the personage at the head of the
stables ; the prince had word of John's disgrace,
remonstrated with him **very** kindly, generously
reinstated him, and bade him promise to sin no
more—a promise which John kept. Another
story is very fondly told of the prince as a young
man hearing of an officer's family in distress, and
how he straightway borrowed six or eight hundred
pounds, put his long fair hair under his hat, and
so disguised carried the money to the starving
family. He sent money, too, to Sheridan on his
death-bed, and would have sent more had not
death ended the career of that man of genius.
Besides these, there are a few pretty speeches,

kind and graceful, to persons with whom he was
brought in contact. But he turned upon twenty
friends. He was fond and familiar with them one
day, and he passed them on the next without
recognition. He used them, liked them, loved
them perhaps in his way, and then separated from
them. On Monday he kissed and fondled poor
Perdita, and on Tuesday he met her and did not
know her. On Wednesday he was very affectionate
with that wretched Brummell, and on Thursday
forgot him; cheated him even out of a snuff-box
which he owed the poor dandy; saw him years
afterwards in his downfall and poverty, when the
bankrupt Beau sent him another snuff-box with
some of the snuff he used to love, as a piteous
token of remembrance and submission, and the
king took the snuff, and ordered his horses and
drove on, and had not the grace to notice his old
companion, favourite, rival, enemy, superior. In
Wraxall there is some gossip about him. When
the charming, beautiful, generous Duchess of
Devonshire died—the lovely lady whom he used
to call his dearest duchess once, and pretend to
admire as all English society admired her—he
said, " Then we have lost the best bred woman in

England," " Then we have lost the kindest heart
in England," said noble Charles Fox.   On another occasion, when three noblemen were to
receive the Garter, says Wraxall, " A great personage observed that never did three men receive
the order in so characteristic a manner.   The
Duke of A. advanced to the sovereign with a
phlegmatic, cold, awkward air like a clown;
Lord B. came forward fawning and smiling like a
courtier; Lord C. presented himself easy, unem-
barrassed, like a gentleman!"   These are the
stories one has to recall about the prince and
king—kindness to a housemaid, generosity to a
groom, criticism on a bow.   There *are* no better
stories about him : they are mean and trivial, and
they characterize him.   The great war of empires
and giants goes on.   Day by day victories are
won and lost by the brave.   Torn, smoky flags
and battered eagles are wrenched from the heroic
enemy and laid at his feet ; and he sits there on
his throne and smiles, and gives the guerdon of
valour to the conqueror.   He ! Elliston the actor,
when the *Coronation* was performed, in which he
took the principal part, used to fancy himself the
king, burst into tears, and hiccup a blessing on

the people. I believe it is certain about George IV., that he had heard so much of the war, knighted so many people, and worn such a prodigious quantity of marshal's uniforms, cocked-hats, cock's feathers, scarlet and bullion in general, that he actually fancied he had been present in some campaigns, and, under the name of General Brock, led a tremendous charge of the German legion at Waterloo.

He is dead but thirty years, and one asks how a great society could have tolerated him ? Would we bear him now ? In this quarter of a century, what a silent revolution has been working! how it has separated us from old times and manners! How it has changed men themselves ! I can see old gentlemen now among us, of perfect good breeding, of quiet lives, with venerable grey heads, fondling their grandchildren ; and look at them, and wonder at what they were once. That gentleman of the grand old school, when he was in the 10th Hussars, and dined at the prince's table, would fall under it night after night. Night after night, that gentleman sate at Brookes's or Raggett's over the dice. If, in the petulance of play or drink, that gentleman spoke a sharp word to his neighbour, he and the other would infallibly go out and try to shoot each other the next morning. That gentleman would drive his friend Richmond the black boxer down to Moulsey, and hold his coat, and shout and swear, and hurrah with delight, whilst the black man was beating Dutch Sam the Jew. That gentleman would take a manly pleasure in pulling his own coat off, and thrashing a barge-man in a street row. That gentleman has been in a watchhouse. That gentleman, so exquisitely polite with ladies in a drawing-room, so loftily courteous, if he talked now as he used among men in his youth, would swear so as to make your hair stand on end. I met lately a very old German gentleman, who had served in our army at the beginning of the century. Since then he has lived on his own estate, but rarely meeting with an Englishman, whose language—the language of fifty years ago that is—he possesses perfectly. When this highly bred old man began to speak English to me, almost every other word he uttered was an oath: as they used it (they swore dreadfully in Flanders) with the Duke of York before Valenciennes, or at Carlton House

over the supper and cards. Read Byron's letters.
So accustomed is the young man to oaths that he
employs them even in writing to his friends, and
swears by the post. Read his account of the
doings of young men at Cambridge, of the ribald
professors, one of whom "could pour out Greek
like a drunken Helot," and whose excesses surpassed even those of the young men. Read
Matthews' description of the boyish lordling's
housekeeping at Newstead, the skull-cup passed
round, the monk's dresses from the masquerade
warehouse, in which the young scapegraces used
to sit until daylight, chanting appropriate songs
round their wine. "We come to breakfast at
two or three o'clock," Matthews says. "There
are gloves and foils for those who like to amuse
themselves, or we fire pistols at a mark in the
hall, or we worry the wolf." A jolly life truly!
The noble young owner of the mansion writes
about such affairs himself in letters to his friend,
Mr. John Jackson, pugilist, in London.

All the prince's time tells a similar strange
story of manners and pleasure. In Wraxall we
find the prime minister himself, the redoubted
William Pitt, engaged in high jinks with person-

ages of no less importance than Lord Thurlow the lord chancellor, and Mr. Dundas the treasurer of the navy. Wraxall relates how these three statesmen, returning after dinner from Addiscombe, found a turnpike open and galloped through it without paying the toll. The turnpike man, fancying they were highwaymen, fired a blunderbuss after them, but missed them; and the poet sang,—

" How as Pitt wandered darkling o'er the plain,
His reason drown'd in Jenkinson's champagne,
A rustic's hand, but righteous fate withstood,
Had shed a premier's for a robber's blood."

Here we have the treasurer of the navy, the lord high chancellor, and the prime minister, all engaged in a most undoubted lark. In Eldon's *Memoirs*, about the very same time, I read that the bar loved wine, as well as the woolsack. Not John Scott himself; he was a good boy always; and though he loved port wine, loved his business and his duty and his fees a great deal better.

He has a Northern Circuit story of those days, about a party at the house of a certain Lawyer Fawcett, who gave a dinner every year to the counsel.

" On one occasion," related Lord Eldon, " I heard Lee say, ' I cannot leave Fawcett's wine. Mind, Davenport, you will go home immediately after dinner, to read the brief in that cause that we have to conduct to-morrow.' "

" ' Not I,' said Davenport. ' Leave my dinner and my wine to read a brief! No, no, Lee; that won't do.'

" ' Then,' said Lee, ' what is to be done? who else is employed?'

" *Davenport.*—' Oh! young Scott.'

" *Lee.*—' Oh! he must go. Mr. Scott, you must go home immediately, and make yourself acquainted with that cause, before our consultation this evening.'

" This was very hard upon me; but I did go, and there was an attorney from Cumberland, and one from Northumberland, and I do not know how many other persons. Pretty late, in came Jack Lee, as drunk as he could be.

" ' I cannot consult to-night; I must go to bed,' he exclaimed, and away he went. Then came Sir Thomas Davenport.

" ' We cannot have a consultation to-night, Mr. Wordsworth ' (Wordsworth, I think, was

the name; it was a Cumberland name), shouted
Davenport. 'Don't you see how drunk Mr. Scott
is? it is impossible to consult.' Poor me! who
had scarce had any dinner, and lost all my wine
—I was so drunk that I could not consult! Well,
a verdict was given against us, and it was all
owing to Lawyer Fawcett's dinner. We moved
for a new trial; and I must say, for the honour
of the bar, that those two gentlemen, Jack **Lee**
and Sir Thomas Davenport, paid all the expenses
between them of the first trial. It is the only
instance I ever knew, but they did. We moved
for a new trial (on the ground, I suppose, of
the counsel not being in their senses), and it was
granted. When it came on, the following year,
the judge rose and said,—

" ' Gentlemen, did any of you dine with
Lawyer Fawcett yesterday? for, if you did, I
will not hear this cause till next year.'

" There was great laughter. We gained the
cause that time."

On another occasion, at Lancaster, where poor
Bozzy **must** needs be going the Northern Circuit,
" we found him," says Mr. Scott, " lying upon
the pavement inebriated. We subscribed a guinea

at supper for him, and a half-crown for his clerk"
—(no doubt there was a large bar, and that
Scott's joke did not cost him much),—"and
sent him, when he waked next morning, a brief,
with instructions to move for what we denominated the writ of *quare adhæsit pavimento?* with
observations duly calculated to induce him to
think that it required great learning to explain
the necessity of granting it, to the judge before
whom he was to move." Boswell sent all round
the town to attorneys for books, that might
enable him to distinguish himself—but in vain.
He moved, however, for the writ, making the best
use he could of the observations in the brief.
The judge was perfectly astonished, and the
audience amazed. The judge said, "I never
heard of such a writ—what can it be that adheres
pavimento? Are any of you gentlemen at the bar
able to explain this?"

The bar laughed. At last one of them said,—

"My lord, Mr. Boswell last night *adhæsit pavimento.* There was no moving him for some time.
At last he was carried to bed, and he has been
dreaming about himself and the pavement."

The canny old gentleman relishes these jokes.

When the Bishop of Lincoln was moving from the deanery of St. Paul's, he says he asked a learned friend of his, by name Will Hay, how he should move some especially fine claret, about which he was anxious.

"Pray, my lord bishop," says Hay, "how much of the wine have you?"

The bishop said six dozen.

"If that is all," Hay answered, "you have but to ask me six times to dinner, and I will carry it all away myself."

There were giants in those days; but this joke about wine is not so fearful as one perpetrated by Orator Thelwall, in the heat of the French Revolution, ten years later, over a frothing pot of porter. He blew the head off, and said, "This is the way I would serve all kings."

Now we come to yet higher personages, and find their doings recorded in the blushing pages of timid little Miss Burney's *Memoirs*. She represents a prince of the blood in quite a royal condition. The loudness, the bigness, boisterousness, creaking boots and rattling oaths, of the young princes, appeared to have frightened the prim household of Windsor, and set all the tea-cups twittering on the tray. On the night of a ball and birthday, when one of the pretty, kind princesses was to come out, it was agreed that her brother, Prince William Henry, should dance the opening minuet with her, and he came to visit the household at their dinner.

"At dinner, Mrs. Schwellenberg presided, attired magnificently; Miss Goldsworthy, Mrs. Stanforth, Messrs. Du Luc and Stanhope, dined with us; and while we were still eating fruit, the Duke of Clarence entered.

"He was just risen from the king's table, and waiting for his equipage to go home and prepare for the ball. To give you an idea of the energy of his royal highness's language, I ought to set apart an objection to writing, or rather intimating, certain forcible words, and beg leave to show you in genuine colours a royal sailor.

"We all rose, of course, upon his entrance, and the two gentlemen placed themselves behind their chairs, while the footmen left the room. But he ordered us all to sit down, and called the men back to hand about some wine. He was in exceeding high spirits, and in the utmost good humour. He placed himself at the head of the table, next Mrs. Schwellenberg, and looked remarkably well, gay, and full of sport and mischief; yet clever withal, as well as comical.

" ' Well, this is the first day I have ever dined with the king at St. James's on his birthday. Pray, have you all drunk his majesty's health ?'

" ' No, your royal highness; your royal highness might make dem do dat,' said Mrs. Schwellenberg.

" ' Oh, by——, I will! Here, you (to the footman), bring champagne; I'll drink the king's health again, if I die for it. Yes, I have done it pretty well already; so has the king, I promise you! I believe his majesty was never taken such good care of before; we have kept his spirits up, I promise you; we have enabled him to go through his fatigues; and I should have done more still, but for the ball and Mary;—I have promised to dance with Mary. I must keep sober for Mary.' "

Indefatigable Miss Burney continues for a dozen pages reporting H.R.H.'s conversation, and indicating, with a humour not unworthy of the clever little author of *Evelina*, the increasing state of excitement of the young sailor prince, who drank more and more champagne, stopped old Mrs. Schwellenberg's remonstrances by giving the old lady a kiss, and telling her to hold her potato-trap, and who did not "keep sober for Mary." Mary had to find another partner that night, for the royal William Henry could not keep his legs.

Will you have a picture of the amusements of another royal prince? It is the Duke of York, the blundering general, the beloved commander-in-chief of the army, the brother with whom George IV. had had many a midnight carouse, and who continued his habits of pleasure almost till death seized his stout body.

In Pückler Muskau's *Letters*, that German prince describes a bout with H.R.H., who in his best time was such a powerful toper that "six bottles of claret after dinner scarce made a perceptible change in his countenance."

"I remember," says Pückler, "that one evening,—indeed, it was past midnight,—he took some of his guests, among whom were the Austrian ambassador, Count Meervelt, Count Beroldingen, and myself, into his beautiful armoury. We tried to swing several Turkish sabres, but none of us had a very firm grasp; whence it happened that the duke and Meervelt both scratched themselves with a sort of straight Indian sword so as to draw blood. Meervelt then wished to try if the sword cut as well as a Damascus, and attempted to cut through one of the wax candles that stood on the table. The experiment answered so ill, that both the candles, candlesticks and all, fell to the ground and were extinguished. While we were groping in the dark and trying to find the door, the duke's aide-de-camp stammered out in great agitation, 'By G—, sir, I remember the sword is poisoned!'

"You may conceive the agreeable feelings of the wounded at this intelligence! Happily, on further examination, it appeared that claret, and not poison, was at the bottom of the colonel's exclamation."

And now I have one more story of the bacchanalian sort, in which Clarence and York, and the very highest personage of the realm, the great Prince Regent, all play parts. The feast took place at the Pavilion at Brighton, and was described to me by a gentleman who was present at the scene. In Gilray's caricatures, and amongst

Fox's jolly associates, there figures a great nobleman, the Duke of Norfolk, called Jockey of
Norfolk in his time, and celebrated for his table
exploits. He had quarrelled with the prince, like
the rest of the Whigs; but a sort of reconcilia-
tion had taken place; and now, being a very old
man, the prince invited him to dine and sleep at
the Pavilion, and the old duke drove over from
his Castle of Arundel with his famous equipage
of grey horses, still remembered in Sussex.

The Prince of Wales had concocted with his
royal brothers a notable scheme for making the
old man drunk. Every person at table was
enjoined to drink wine with the duke—a challenge
which the old toper did not refuse. He soon
began to see that there was a conspiracy against
him; he drank glass for glass; he overthrew
many of the brave. At last the First Gentleman
of Europe proposed bumpers of brandy. One of
the royal brothers filled a great glass for the
duke. He stood up and tossed off the drink.
"Now," says he, "I will have my carriage, and
go home." The prince urged upon him his pre-
vious promise to sleep under the roof where he
had been so generously entertained. "No," he

said, he had had enough of such hospitality.
A trap had been set for him; he would leave
the place at once and never enter its doors
more.

The carriage was called, and came; but, in the
half-hour's interval, the liquor had proved too
potent for the old man; his host's generous
purpose was answered, and the duke's old grey
head lay stupefied on the table. Nevertheless,
when his post-chaise was announced, he staggered
to it as well as he could, and stumbling in, bade
the postilions drive to Arundel. They drove him
for half an hour round and round the Pavilion
lawn; the poor old man fancied he was going
home. When he awoke that morning he was
in bed at the prince's hideous house at Brighton.
You may see the place now for sixpence: they
have fiddlers there every day; and sometimes
buffoons and mountebanks hire the Riding House
and do their tricks and tumbling there. The
trees are still there, and the gravel walks round
which the poor old sinner was trotted. I can
fancy the flushed faces of the royal princes as
they support themselves at the portico pillars,
and look on at old Norfolk's disgrace; but I can't

fancy how the man who perpetrated it continued to be called a gentleman.

From drinking, the pleased Muse now turns to gambling, of which in his youth our prince was a great practitioner. He was a famous pigeon for the play-men; they lived upon him. Egalité Orleans, it was believed, punished him severely. A noble lord, whom we shall call the Marquis of Steyne, is said to have mulcted him in immense sums. He frequented the clubs, where play was then almost universal; and, as it was known his debts of honour were sacred, whilst he was gambling Jews waited outside to purchase his notes of hand. His transactions on the turf were unlucky as well as discreditable : though I believe he, and his jockey, and his horse Escape, were all innocent in that affair which created so much scandal.

Arthur's, Almack's, Bootle's, and White's were the chief clubs of the young men of fashion. There was play at all, and decayed noblemen and broken-down senators fleeced the unwary there. In Selwyn's *Letters* we find Carlisle, Devonshire, Coventry, Queensberry, all undergoing the probation. Charles Fox, a dreadful gambler, was

cheated in very late times—lost 200,000*l*. at play.
Gibbon tells of his playing for twenty-two hours
at a sitting, and losing 500*l*. an hour. That
indomitable punter said that the greatest pleasure
in life, after winning, was losing. What hours,
what nights, what health did he waste over the
devil's books! I was going to say what peace of
mind; but he took his losses very philosophically.
After an awful night's play, and the enjoyment
of the greatest pleasure but *one* in life, he was
found on a sofa tranquilly reading an Eclogue of
Virgil.

Play survived long after the wild prince and
Fox had given up the dice-box. The dandies
continued it. Byron, Brummell—how many
names could I mention of men of the world who
have suffered by it! In 1837 occurred a famous
trial which pretty nigh put an end to gambling in
England. A peer of the realm was found cheat-
ing at whist, and repeatedly seen to practise the
trick called *sauter la coupe*. His friends at the
clubs saw him cheat, and went on playing with
him. One greenhorn, who had discovered his
foul play, asked an old hand what he should do.
"Do," said the Mammon of Unrighteousness,

"*Back him, you fool.*" The best efforts were
made to screen him. People wrote him anony-
mous letters and warned him ; but he would
cheat, and they were obliged to find him out.
Since that day, when my lord's shame was made
public, the gaming-table has lost all its splendour.
Shabby Jews and blacklegs prowl about race-
courses and tavern parlours, and now and then
inveigle silly yokels with greasy packs of cards
in railroad cars ; but Play is a deposed goddess,
her worshippers bankrupt and her table in rags.

So is another famous British institution gone
to decay—the Ring : the noble practice of British
boxing, which in my youth was still almost
flourishing.

The prince, in his early days, was a great
patron of this national sport, as his grand-uncle
Culloden Cumberland had been before him ; but,
being present at a fight at Brighton, where one
of the combatants was killed, the prince pen-
sioned the boxer's widow, and declared he never
would attend another battle. "But, nevertheless,"—I read in the noble language of Pierce
Egan (whose smaller work on Pugilism I have
the honour to possess),—"he thought it a manly

and decided English feature, which ought not
to be destroyed. His majesty had a drawing of the
sporting characters in the Fives' Court placed in
his boudoir, to remind him of his former attachment and support of true courage; and when any
fight of note occurred after he was king, accounts
of it were read to him by his desire." That
gives one a fine image of a king taking his
recreation;—at ease in a royal dressing-gown;—
too majestic to read himself, ordering the prime
minister to read him accounts of battles: how
Cribb punched Molyneux's eye, or Jack Randall
thrashed the Game Chicken.

Where my prince *did* actually distinguish himself was in driving. He drove once in four hours
and a half from Brighton to Carlton House—
fifty-six miles. All the young men of that day
were fond of that sport. But the fashion of
rapid driving deserted England; and, I believe,
trotted over to America. Where are the amusements of our youth? I hear of no gambling
now but amongst obscure ruffians; of no boxing
but amongst the lowest rabble. One solitary
four-in-hand still drove round the parks in London last year; but that charioteer must soon

disappear. He was very old ; he was attired after
the fashion of the year 1825. He must drive to
the banks of Styx ere long,—where the ferry-boat
waits to carry him over to the defunct revellers,
who boxed and gambled and drank and drove
with King George.

The bravery of the Brunswicks, that all the
family must have it, that George possessed it, are
points which all English writers have agreed to
admit ; and yet I cannot see how George IV.
should have been endowed with this quality.
Swaddled in feather-beds all his life, lazy, obese,
perpetually eating and drinking, his education
was quite unlike that of his tough old progenitors.
His grandsires had confronted hardship and war,
and ridden up and fired their pistols undaunted
into the face of death. His father had conquered
luxury, and overcome indolence. Here was one
who never resisted any temptation ; never had a
desire but he coddled and pampered it ; if ever he
had any nerve, frittered it away among cooks, and
tailors, and barbers, and furnituremongers, and
opera dancers. What muscle would not grow
flaccid in such a life—a life that was never strung
up to any action—an endless Capua without any

campaign—all fiddling, and flowers, and feasting, and flattery, and folly? When George III. was pressed by the Catholic question and the India Bill, he said he would retire to Hanover rather than yield upon either point; and he would have done what he said. But, before yielding, he was determined to fight his ministers and parliament; and he did, and he beat them. The time came when George IV. was pressed too upon the Catholic claims: the cautious Peel had slipped over to that side; the grim old Wellington had joined it; and Peel tells us, in his *Memoirs*, what was the conduct of the king. He at first refused to submit; whereupon Peel and the duke offered their resignations, which their gracious master accepted. He did these two gentlemen the honour, Peel says, to kiss them both when they went away. (Fancy old Arthur's grim countenance and eagle beak as the monarch kisses it!) When they were gone he sent after them, surrendered, and wrote to them a letter begging them to remain in office, and allowing them to have their way. Then his majesty had a meeting with Eldon, which is related at curious length in the latter's *Memoirs*. He told Eldon what was not true about his interview with the new Catholic converts; utterly misled the old ex-chancellor; cried, whimpered, fell on his neck, and kissed him too. We know old Eldon's own tears were pumped very freely. Did these two fountains gush together? I can't fancy a behaviour more unmanly, imbecile, pitiable. This a defender of the faith! This a chief in the crisis of a great nation! This an inheritor of the courage of the Georges!

Many of my hearers no doubt have journeyed to the pretty old town of Brunswick, in company with that most worthy, prudent, and polite gentleman, the Earl of Malmesbury, and fetched away Princess Caroline for her longing husband, the Prince of Wales. Old Queen Charlotte would have had her eldest son marry a niece of her own, that famous Louisa of Strelitz, afterwards Queen of Prussia, and who shares with Marie Antoinette in the last age the sad pre-eminence of beauty and misfortune. But George III. had a niece at Brunswick: she was a richer princess than her Serene Highness of Strelitz:—in fine, the Princess Caroline was selected to marry the heir to the English throne. We follow my Lord Malmesbury in quest of her; we are introduced to her illus-

trious father and royal mother; we witness the
balls and fêtes of the old court ; we are presented
to the princess herself, with her fair hair, her
blue eyes, and her impertinent shoulders—a lively,
bouncing, romping princess, who takes the advice
of her courtly English mentor most generously
and kindly. We can be present at her very
toilette, if we like, regarding which, and for very
good reasons, the British courtier implores her to
be particular. What a strange court ! What a
queer privacy of morals and manners do we look
into ! Shall we regard it as preachers and
moralists, and cry, Woe, against the open vice and
selfishness and corruption ; or look at it as we do
at the king in the pantomime, with his pantomime
wife, and pantomime courtiers, whose big heads
he knocks together, whom he pokes with his pantomime sceptre, whom he orders to prison under
the guard of his pantomime beefeaters, as he sits
down to dine on his pantomime pudding ? It
is grave, it is sad, it is theme most curious
for moral and political speculation; it is monstrous, grotesque, laughable, with its prodigious littlenesses, etiquettes, ceremonials, sham
moralities; it is as serious as a sermon, and

as absurd and outrageous as Punch's puppet-show.

Malmesbury tells us of the private life of the duke, Princess Caroline's father, who was to die, like his warlike son, in arms against the French; presents us to his courtiers, his favourite; his duchess, George III.'s sister, a grim old princess, who took the British envoy aside, and told him wicked old stories of wicked old dead people and times; who came to England afterwards when her nephew was regent, and lived in a shabby furnished lodging, old, and dingy, and deserted, and grotesque, but somehow royal. And we go with him to the duke to demand the princess's hand in form, and we hear the Brunswick guns fire their adieux of salute, as H.R.H. the Princess of Wales departs in the frost and snow; and we visit the domains of the Prince Bishop of Osna-burg—the Duke of York of our early time; and we dodge about from the French revolutionists, whose ragged legions are pouring over Holland and Germany, and gaily trampling down the old world to the tune of *ça ira;* and we take shipping at Slade, and we land at Greenwich, where the princess's ladies and the prince's ladies are in waiting to receive her royal highness.

What a history follows! Arrived in London, the bridegroom hastened eagerly to receive his bride. When she was first presented to him, Lord Malmesbury says she very properly attempted to kneel. He raised her gracefully enough, embraced her, and turning round to me, said,—

" Harris, I am not well; pray get me a glass of brandy."

I said, " Sir, had you not better have a glass of water?"

Upon which, much out of humour, he said, with an oath, " No; I will go to the queen."

What could be expected from a wedding which had such a beginning—from such a bridegroom and such a bride? I am not going to carry you through the scandal of that story, or follow the poor princess through all her vagaries; her balls and her dances, her travels to Jerusalem and Naples, her jigs, and her junketings, and her tears. As I read her trial in history, I vote she is not guilty. I don't say it is an impartial verdict; but as one reads her story the heart bleeds for the kindly, generous, outraged creature. If wrong

there be, let it lie at his door who wickedly thrust
her from it. Spite of her follies, the great,
hearty people of England loved, and protected,

The Prince and Princess of Wales.

and pitied her. " God bless you! we will bring
your husband back to you," said a mechanic one
day, as she told Lady Charlotte Bury with tears

14—2

streaming down her cheeks. They could not bring that husband back ; they could not cleanse that selfish heart. Was hers the only one he had wounded ? Steeped in selfishness, impotent for faithful attachment and manly enduring love,— had it not survived remorse, was it not accustomed to desertion ?

Malmesbury gives us the beginning of the marriage story ;—how the prince reeled into chapel to be married ; how he hiccupped out his vows of fidelity—you know how he kept them ; how he pursued the woman whom he had married ; to what a state he brought her ; with what blows he struck her ; with what malignity he pursued her ; what his treatment of his daughter was ; and what his own life. *He* the first gentleman of Europe ! There is no stronger satire on the proud English society of that day, than that they admired George.

No, thank God, we can tell of better gentlemen ; and whilst our eyes turn away, shocked, from this monstrous image of pride, vanity, weakness, they may see in that England over which the last George pretended to reign, some who merit indeed the title of gentlemen, some who make our hearts beat when we hear their names, and whose memory we fondly salute when that of yonder imperial manikin is tumbled into oblivion. I will take men of my own profession of letters. I will take Walter Scott, who loved the king, and who was his sword and buckler, and championed him like that brave Highlander in his own story, who fights round his craven chief. What a good gentleman! What a friendly soul, what a generous hand, what an amiable life was that of the noble Sir Walter! I will take another man of letters, whose life I admire even more,—an English worthy, doing his duty for fifty noble years of labour, day by day storing up learning, day by day working for scant wages, most charitable out of his small means, bravely faithful to the calling which he had chosen, refusing to turn from his path for popular praise or princes' favour;—I mean *Robert Southey*. We have left his old political landmarks miles and miles behind; we protest against his dogmatism; nay, we begin to forget it and his politics: but I hope his life will not be forgotten, for it is sublime in its simplicity, its energy, its honour, its affection. In the combat between Time and Thalaba, I suspect the

former destroyer has conquered. Kehama's curse
frightens very few readers now; but Southey's
private letters are worth piles of epics, and are
sure to last among us, as long as kind hearts like
to sympathize with goodness and purity, and love
and upright life. " If your feelings are like
mine," he writes to his wife, " I will not go to
Lisbon without you, or I will stay at home, and
not part from you. For though not unhappy
when away, still without you I am not happy.
For your sake, as well as my own and little
Edith's, I will not consent to any separation; the
growth of a year's love between her and me, if it
please God she should live, is a thing too delightful in itself, and too valuable in its consequences,
to be given up for any light inconvenience on
your part or mine. . . . On these things we
will talk at leisure; only, dear, dear Edith, *we
must not part!*"

This was a poor literary gentleman. The First
Gentleman in Europe had a wife and daughter
too. Did he love them so? Was he faithful to
them? Did he sacrifice ease for them, or show
them the sacred examples of religion and honour?
Heaven gave the Great English Prodigal no such

good fortune. Peel proposed to make a baronet of Southey; and to this advancement the king agreed. The poet nobly rejected the offered promotion.

" I have," he wrote, " a pension of 200l. a year, conferred upon me by the good offices of my old friend C. Wynn, and I have the laureateship. The salary of the latter was immediately appropriated, as far as it went, to a life insurance for 3,000l., which, with an earlier insurance, is the sole provision I have made for my family. All beyond must be derived from my own industry. Writing for a livelihood, a livelihood is all that I have gained; for, having also something better in view, and never, therefore, having courted popularity, nor written for the mere sake of gain, it has not been possible for me to lay by anything. Last year, for the first time in my life, I was provided with a year's expenditure beforehand. This exposition may show how unbecoming and unwise it would be to accept the rank which, so greatly to my honour, you have solicited for me."

How noble his poverty is, compared to the wealth of his master! His acceptance even of a pension was made the object of his opponents'

satire : but think of the merit and modesty of
this State pensioner; and that other enormous
drawer of public money, who receives 100,000*l.*
a year, and comes to Parliament with a request
for 650,000*l.* more!

Another true knight of those days was Cuth-
bert Collingwood; and I think, since heaven
made gentlemen, there is no record of a better
one than that. Of brighter deeds, I grant you,
we may read performed by others; but where of
a nobler, kinder, more beautiful life of duty, of a
gentler, truer heart? Beyond dazzle of success
and blaze of genius, I fancy shining a hundred
and a hundred times higher, the sublime purity of
Collingwood's gentle glory. His heroism stirs
British hearts when we recall it. His love, and
goodness, and piety make one thrill with happy
emotion. As one reads of him and his great com-
rade going into the victory with which their names
are immortally connected, how the old English
word comes up, and that old English feeling of
what I should like to call Christian honour!
What gentlemen they were, what great hearts
they had! "We can, my dear Coll," writes
Nelson to him, "have no little jealousies; we

have only one great object in view,—that of meeting the enemy, and getting a glorious peace for our country." At Trafalgar, when the *Royal Sovereign* was pressing alone into the midst of the combined fleets, Lord Nelson said to Captain Blackwood: " See how that noble fellow, Collingwood, takes his ship into action! How I envy him!" The very same throb and impulse of heroic generosity was beating in Collingwood's honest bosom. As he led into the fight, he said: " What would Nelson give to be here!"

After the action of the 1st of June, he writes:— " We cruised for a few days, like disappointed people looking for what they could not find, *until the morning of little Sarah's birthday*, between eight and nine o'clock, when the French fleet of twenty-five sale of the line, was discovered to windward. We chased them, and they bore down within about five miles of us. The night was spent in watching and preparation for the succeeding day; and many a blessing did I send forth to my Sarah, lest I should never bless her more. At dawn, we made our approach on the enemy, then drew up, dressed our ranks, and it was about eight when the admiral made the signal for each

ship to engage her opponent, and bring her to
close action; and then down we went under a
crowd of sail, and in a manner that would have
animated the coldest heart, and struck terror into
the most intrepid enemy. The ship we were to
engage was two ahead of the French admiral, so
we had to go through his fire and that of two ships
next to him, and received all their broadsides two
or three times, before we fired a gun. It was
then near ten o'clock. I observed to the admiral,
that about that time our wives were going to
church, but that I thought the peal we should
ring about the Frenchman's ears would outdo
their parish bells."

There are no words to tell what the heart feels
in reading the simple phrases of such a hero.
Here is victory and courage, but love sublimer
and superior. Here is a Christian soldier spend-
ing the night before battle in watching and pre-
paring for the succeeding day, thinking of his
dearest home, and sending many blessings forth
to his Sarah, "lest he should never bless her
more." Who would not say Amen to his sup-
plication? It was a benediction to his country—
the prayer of that intrepid loving heart.

We have spoken of a good soldier and good men of letters as specimens of English gentlemen of the age just past : may we not also—many of my elder hearers, I am sure, have read, and fondly remember his delightful story—speak of a good divine, and mention Reginald Heber as one of the best of English gentlemen ? The charming poet, the happy possessor of all sorts of gifts and accomplishments, birth, wit, fame, high character, competence—he was the beloved parish priest in his own home of Hoderel, " counselling his people in their troubles, advising them in their difficulties, comforting them in distress, kneeling often at their sick beds at the hazard of his own life ; exhorting, encouraging where there was need ; where there was strife the peacemaker ; where there was want the free giver."

When the Indian bishopric was offered to him he refused at first ; but after communing with himself (and committing his case to the quarter whither such pious men are wont to carry their doubts), he withdrew his refusal, and prepared himself for his mission and to leave his beloved parish. "Little children, love one another, and forgive one another," were the last sacred words he said to his weeping people. He parted with them, knowing, perhaps, he should see them no more. Like those other good men of whom we have just spoken, **love** and duty were **his life's** aim. Happy **he**, happy they who were so gloriously faithful to both! He writes to his wife those charming lines on his journey :—

" If thou, my love, wert by my side, my babies at my knee,
  How gladly would our pinnace glide o'er Gunga's mimic sea!

  I miss thee at the dawning gray, when, on our deck reclined,
  In careless ease my limbs I lay and woo the cooler wind.

  I miss thee when by Gunga's stream my twilight steps I guide;
  But most beneath the lamp's pale beam I miss thee by my
      side.

  I spread my books, my pencil try, the lingering noon to cheer;
  But miss thy kind approving eye, thy meek attentive ear.

  But when of morn and eve the star beholds me on my knee,
  I feel, though thou art distant far, thy prayers ascend for me.

  Then on! then on! where duty leads my course be onward
      still,—
  O'er broad Hindostan's sultry meads, o'er bleak Almorah's
      hill.

  That course nor Delhi's kingly gates, nor wild Malwah detain,
  For sweet the bliss us both awaits by yonder western main.

  Thy towers, Bombay, gleam bright, they say, across the dark
      blue sea :
  But ne'er were hearts so blithe and gay as there shall meet
      in thee ! "

Is it not Collingwood and Sarah, and Southey and Edith? His affection is part of his life. What were life without it? Without love, I can fancy no gentleman.

How touching is a remark Heber makes in his *Travels through India*, that on inquiring of the natives at a town, which of the governors of India stood highest in the opinion of the people, he found that, though Lord Wellesley and Warren **Hastings were** honoured as the two greatest men who had ever ruled this part of the world, the people spoke with chief affection of Judge Cleaveland, **who had** died, aged twenty-nine, in 1784. The people have built a monument over him, and still hold a religious feast in his memory. **So** does his own country still tend with a heart's regard the memory of the gentle Heber.

And Cleaveland died in 1784, and is still loved by the heathen, is he? Why, that year 1784 was remarkable in the **life** of our friend the First Gentleman of Europe. Do you not know that he was twenty-one in that year, and opened Carlton House with a grand ball to the nobility and gentry, and doubtless wore that lovely pink coat which we have described. I was eager to read

about the ball, and looked to the old magazines
for information. The entertainment took place
on the 10th February. In the *European Magazine* of March, 1784, I came straightway
upon it :—

"The alterations at Carlton House being
finished, we lay before our readers a description
of the state apartments as they appeared on the
10th instant, when H.R.H. gave a grand ball to
the principal nobility and gentry. .. . .
The entrance to the state room fills the mind
with an inexpressible idea of greatness and
splendour.

"The state chair is of a gold frame, covered
with crimson damask ; on each corner of the feet
is a lion's head, expressive of fortitude and
strength ; the feet of the chair have serpents
twining round them, to denote wisdom. Facing
the throne, appears the helmet of Minerva; and
over the windows, glory is represented by Saint
George with a superb gloria.

"But the saloon may be styled the *chef
d'œuvre*, and in every ornament discovers great
invention. It is hung with a figured lemon satin.
The window-curtains, sofas, and chairs are of the

same colour. The ceiling is ornamented with emblematical paintings, representing the Graces and Muses, together with Jupiter, Mercury, Apollo, and Paris. Two *ormolu* chandeliers are placed here. It is impossible by expression to do justice to the extraordinary workmanship, as well as design, of the ornaments. They each consist of a palm, branching out in five directions for the reception of lights. A beautiful figure of a rural nymph is represented entwining the stems of the tree with wreaths of flowers. In the centre of the room is a rich chandelier. To see this apartment *dans son plus beau jour*, it should be viewed in the glass over the chimney-piece. The range of apartments from the saloon to the ball-room, when the doors are open, formed one of the grandest spectacles that ever was beheld."

In the *Gentleman's Magazine*, for the very same month and year—March, 1784—is an account of another festival, in which another great gentleman of English extraction is represented as taking a principal share :—

" According to order, H. E. the Commander-in-Chief was admitted to a public audience of Congress; and, being seated, the president, after a pause, informed him that the United States assembled were ready to receive his communications. Whereupon he arose, and spoke as follows :—

" 'Mr. President,—The great events on which my resignation depended having at length taken place, I present myself before Congress to surrender into their hands the trust committed to me, and to claim the indulgence of retiring from the service of my country.

" 'Happy in the confirmation of our independence and sovereignty, I resign the appointment I accepted with diffidence; which, however, was superseded by a confidence in the rectitude of our cause, the support of the supreme power of the nation, and the patronage of Heaven. I close this last act of my official life, by commending the interests of our dearest country to the protection of Almighty God, and those who have the superintendence of them to His holy keeping. Having finished the work assigned me, I retire from the great theatre of action; and, bidding an affectionate farewell to this august body, under whose orders I have so long acted, I here offer my commission and take my leave of the employ-

ments of my public life.' To which the president
replied :—

" ' Sir, having defended the standard of liberty
in the New World, having taught a lesson useful
to those who inflict and those who feel oppres-
sion, you retire with the blessings of your fellow-
citizens; though the glory of your virtues will
not terminate with your military command, but
will descend to remotest ages.' "

Which was the most splendid spectacle ever
witnessed;—the opening feast of Prince George
in London, or the resignation of Washington?
Which is the noble character for after ages to
admire;—yon fribble dancing in lace and spangles,
or yonder hero who sheathes his sword after a
life of spotless honour, a purity unreproached, a
courage indomitable, and a consummate victory?
Which of these is the true gentleman? What
is it to be a gentleman? Is it to have lofty
aims, to lead a pure life, to keep your honour
virgin; to have the esteem of your fellow-citizens,
and the love of your fireside; to bear good
fortune meekly; to suffer evil with constancy;
and through evil or good to maintain truth
always? Show me the happy man whose life

15

exhibits these qualities, and him we will salute as gentleman, whatever his rank may be; show me the prince who possesses them, and he may be sure of our love and loyalty. The heart of Britain still beats kindly for George III.,—not because he was wise and just, but because he was pure in life, honest in intent, and because according to his lights he worshipped heaven. I think we acknowledge in the inheritrix of his sceptre, a wiser rule, and a life as honourable and pure; and I am sure the future painter of our manners will pay a willing allegiance to that good life, and be loyal to the memory of that unsullied virtue.

THE END.